Praise for *Get an Internship and Make the Most of It***:**

"Some very good, realistic tips for young people. Getting a job is becoming more competitive every day. I think, by serving an internship, the student has a definite 'edge' over other students. Internships allow students to experience their career choice in a more relaxed, non-threatening way. Internships give students authentic work experiences that complement their educational experiences. Using Jessica, Luis, Michelle, and Alex in examples . . . personalizes the information and makes it easier to understand."

> —**Cindy Davey**, Business Education Teacher/Work Experience Coordinator, Connecticut

"Seniors would come back from their internships energized. For many it was the chance to be of service. For others it was an 'aha' moment: 'I never thought about working in this area but I really liked it. Now I know what I want to major in at college.' For just about every student it fostered an appreciation of what it was like to be working in what they called 'the real world.' Because the internship at our school was for seniors and came near the end of the senior year it got them out of the building at a time when they were ready to be out. The senior project was the perfect antidote to senior slump."

> —**Doug Wilcock**, Cape Cod Academy

"Joan E. McLachlan and Patricia F. Hess have written a most welcome guide for high school and college students who wish to engage in meaningful internship experiences. Starting with the ABCs of finding a suitable placement, this book offers a step-by-step approach to successful interviewing, as well as developing efficient work habits and realistic expectations of the workplace site. It is chock full of information and encouragement for all types of students, those who are ready to take the plunge and those who are less confident. It is indeed an indispensable primer for getting the most out of internships."

> —**Joan Chabrowe**, former internship coordinator, City-As-School NYC

Get an Internship
and Make the Most of It

Practical Information for High School and Community College Students

Joan E. McLachlan and Patricia F. Hess

ROWMAN & LITTLEFIELD
Lanham • Boulder • New York • London

Published by Rowman & Littlefield
A wholly owned subsidary of The Rowman & Littlefield
Publishing Group, Inc.
4501 Forbes Boulevard, Suite 200, Lanham, Maryland 20706
www.rowman.com

Unit A, Whitacre Mews, 26–34 Stannary Street, London SE11 4AB

British Library Cataloguing in Publication Information Available

Library of Congress Cataloging-in-Publication Data

McLachlan, Joan E., 1943–
Get an internship and make the most of it : practical information for
high school and community college students / Joan E. McLachlan and
Patricia F. Hess.
    pages cm
Includes bibliographical references and index.
ISBN 978-1-4758-1465-1 (cloth : alk. paper)—ISBN 978-1-4758-1466-8
(pbk. : alk. paper)—ISBN 978-1-4758-1467-5 (electronic)
1. Internship programs—United States. 2. High school students—
Employment—United States. 3. Community college students—
Employment—United States. 4. School-to-work transition—United States.
I. Hess, Patricia, 1943– II. Title.
LC1072.I58M349 2015
371.2'27—dc23   2015003968

∞™ The paper used in this publication meets the minimum requirements
of American National Standard for Information Sciences—Permanence of
Paper for Printed Library Materials, ANSI/NISO Z39.48-1992.

Printed in the United States of America

Contents

An Internship for You

Internships are always in the news. You've heard about them from your friends. You've seen stories about students who have done them. And you may be thinking that internships are there only for those Advanced Placement (AP) students, techies, or math and science geniuses. Or just for students who know exactly where they're going. Or just for college grads.

You may have thought, "I just don't have any work experience, so I can't do an internship," or "I have no idea what career I want," or "I don't have any connections in a business or organization."

But internships *are* for you. An internship will help you try out a career and give you some work experience. An internship will help you decide what you may want to do—or not do—in the future.

Or you may be thinking that internships are just working inside in an office.

An internship, sure, can be in an office, but it can also be out in the field with environmental or conservation organizations; local fire, police, or recreational departments; or a landscaping company.

An internship can also be with a community-theater company; a museum; a local newspaper, radio, or TV station; or out on a golf course testing the turf.

There are many, many places that would welcome students as interns.

Okay, we know you've heard those horror stories about interns spending all their time going for coffee or running errands, and you figure, "What a waste of time."

But a good internship is so much more than being a "gofer." A good internship lets you get involved in an organization or company, learn new skills, and do things that add value.

A good internship has a mentor who can help guide you.

Maybe you want to give an internship a try but are not sure what to do next.

This book will help you find, get, and make the most out of an internship that's right for you—the internship that will give you that all-important real-world experience that employers and college admissions value. The internship that will let you

- Test drive a career before you commit to a college major or a job
- Learn new skills
- Build a network of colleagues and
- Take a chance on something new.

Internships are best when they're done through a school or college. Most schools and colleges have internship programs. Let the coordinator or director know that you're interested.

If there is no formal program, tell your school or college that you want to do an internship before you graduate. And if you get nowhere with them, tell them again. Your school or college wants you to succeed. They need you to succeed. If getting that real-world experience will help you get to your future goals, then they will try to make that internship happen.

If you're still getting nowhere, chapters 1 and 2 will give you some other ideas.

Once you know what internship you want, this book will give you tips and techniques on interviewing, show you how to answer those interview questions, and tell you exactly what the interviewer is looking for when she asks you those interview questions.

Once you have that internship, we'll tell you how to get the most out of it. And this includes how to deal with the ups and downs that will come your way.

And, finally, we'll show you how to make sure that your internship experience, whatever it is like, is something you can build on for your future.

So, get going! Get that internship you want now. It will make a big difference in your life and let you make the right decisions for your future.

We wish you all the best as you go forward.

—Joan and Patricia

❶

Find an Internship

Everyone is talking about internships. It used to be that new college graduates would be the ones out there looking for an internship to get experience. But now college students want to get some experience in the real world. High school students want to try out a career area before they commit to a career or college major. And everyone, it seems, wants to beef up their résumés with internship experience.

WHAT ARE THESE INTERNSHIPS EVERYONE'S TALKING ABOUT?

The definition of an internship can vary so much that it's hard to get a clear picture of what it really is. Formally, an internship has been defined as a work-related learning experience that can last anywhere from a few weeks to a semester. The intern arranges the hours and specific days of the internship with the school or college and the sponsoring organization.

But an internship is much more than that. Perhaps the best way to understand what an internship is, is to look at what doing an internship can offer you.

Good internships can give you

- A chance to test drive a career
- A chance to get real-world learning experience
- A chance to meet and learn from people who are actually doing what you might want to do one day

- A chance to build professional relationships
- A chance to develop some skills to take with you for the rest of your life and
- A chance to apply some of what you've learned in the classroom to the world that you'll be moving on to.

The best internships are ones where the school is involved. That way, if there are problems, the school can step in and help sort them out. The school or college is there to give support to both you and the organization or business.

Internships that aren't part of any school or college or organized program—like those found individually after graduation—often don't provide the best experiences. The intern is often on his own and may not get the most from the experience.

So when you start thinking about doing an internship, check with your school or college and try to get involved with an existing program.

INTERNSHIP TERMS

Just a word about some of the terms used when talking about internships.

Some programs refer to the locations that host interns as *sponsors*, *sites*, *organizations*, *businesses*, *placements*, or even *employers*. It doesn't really matter what term is used as long as it's clear that this is the place where the intern will be spending time learning and working for a set period of time.

Supervisors, *mentors*, and *sponsors* are other terms that are sometimes used interchangeably. They all refer to the person who will be working most closely with the intern. In some cases, the supervisor and mentor are two different people. In others, one person performs both roles. Whatever term is used, this is who will be your go-to person throughout your internship.

IS AN INTERNSHIP RIGHT FOR ME?

You may be asking yourself, "Is an internship right for me?"

Consider this: An internship can help you figure out the next steps in your life. It can give you a chance to explore a career that you may have never considered. It can also give you real-world experience in a career field you already like.

An internship will help you build some new skills that employers and colleges want—skills that will help you in that first job interview or college admissions interview.

So when you ask, "Is an internship right for me?" the answer is a resounding *YES!*

I HAVE NO IDEA WHERE TO BEGIN!

It can seem like a royal pain doing the upfront work of deciding on a career area and finding an internship, but if you spend some time thinking about where you want to be for your internship, you'll save a lot of energy and effort in the long run. And it will lead to a more interesting experience than just grabbing at any internship you come across.

If you try to picture yourself actually at work, that may help you think about where you want to intern. Are you in an office? Are you wearing business attire? Are you in a chill, laid-back workplace where everyone is casual, not at workstations, and where meetings are informal? Are you working with a team of people to accomplish a project? Do you have some down time where you can work by yourself quietly? Are you in scrubs in a busy medical placement? Are you outside, working with a field team on an ecological project—up to your elbows in mud?

Your interests and skills are another thing to consider. You may like working with people, or computers, or kids. You may like working mainly outside or with your hands or in a science field. Think about what interests you before you sign on to spend your time at a specific site.

WHERE DO I FIND THESE INTERNSHIPS?

Surprisingly, internships are everywhere. You just have to know where to look.

Use Your School

If you're in school and the school has an internship program, great. See if you can apply and join that program. Some internship programs already have a list of possible internship sponsors that you can select from. Other internship programs require students to locate their own internships, but they usually have lists of businesses and organizations that have hosted interns in the past. If you know what career area you're looking for, ask if there is a site that has been a sponsor before. If you're still unsure, ask if you can talk with someone about what possibilities are available.

If there is no official internship program, ask where the guidance or career center is, and go there. You'll be amazed at the support and information that's offered. Some schools offer this type of help through the business department. Even if there is no formal center, faculty members can be very helpful if you just ask.

Your school or college program may require an internship in your field. Use those contacts to help find the one that's right for you. You might be able to earn academic credit for the work you do if you're part of an official internship program. Getting credit for your efforts makes a lot of the hard work you'll be doing seem more worthwhile because interns often (very often) are not paid or are paid very little.

Networking Works

On your own? Start by networking. Networking means exploring every connection you can think of who might have information or know someone or somewhere willing to offer an internship to you. This means friends, friends of friends, relatives, friends of relatives, teachers, and friends of teachers. As for your family, aunts, uncles, and cousins may know someone who wants an intern. (But don't just tuck into a family business because it is familiar. This is the time to stretch yourself and try new things.)

Let everyone know that you're looking for an internship.

Check Out Your Community

Doing research for an internship placement involves looking at what companies, nonprofits, organizations, or government agencies are in your town or city. Are they doing work that you might like to try? Approach them. If they have a human resources department, send them an e-mail telling them what you're looking for. If it's a small company, send the e-mail to the "boss." You might be surprised to know how many bosses started their career with an internship.

Think big. What are some organizations in which you could build the skills you're interested in developing? For example, if you're interested in helping people, organizations that might offer internships are youth centers, local hospitals, treatment centers, social-services agencies, local churches, and so on. If you're interested in history or anthropology, the local natural-history museum, the local historical society, or a restoration project might provide exposure to various aspects of a curator's or anthropologist's job.

Check out some of these places for listings of possible businesses and internship sites in your area:

- Yellow Pages (Yes, they still exist)
- Local chamber of commerce
- Town or county business websites
- Local Better Business Bureau
- Rotary Clubs
- Not-for-profit organizations
- Local business directories
- Local newspaper business sections (hard copies and online)
- Libraries
- Local government offices

Let your school or college know what you want to do so that you're not alone in getting what you want.

Go for it. You may get just what you need.

NARROW YOUR CHOICES

As much as you'd like to try out everything you've ever dreamed of doing, at some point you're going to have to narrow things down and make a decision. The good thing about an internship is that it doesn't have to be something you'll be doing for the rest of your life. Now is the time to try out what you think might be a possible career before you have to make final decisions. It's like test-driving a car. You don't have to buy it, even if you've taken it for a long drive.

Trust Yourself

Sometimes you know just what you want to do. And sometimes you know what it is that you *don't* want to do.

***

Michelle
Michelle is a senior at Centertown High School. Her guidance counselor has been talking to her all year about going to a four-year college. Michelle is not so sure about this idea, so her guidance counselor suggested she talk to the school's internship coordinator about doing an internship before she graduates.

> *I thought doing an internship was a good idea since I wasn't too sure what I wanted to do after high school. Our internship coordinator started talking about internships in an elementary school. She thought that since I volunteer with the Boys and Girls Club I would like that kind of internship.*
>
> *Actually, that didn't sound so good to me.*
>
> *And then she mentioned one at a hotel nearby that specializes in conferences and weddings. I wanted something different, and that sounded much more interesting.*

Luckily, Michelle's school had an internship program, so it was easy for her to connect with internship opportunities. She also had an idea of what she didn't want to do. She found herself attracted to a field that neither she nor her guidance counselor had even considered.

> **TIP:** Now is the time to take a chance on something different. If you think you'd like to try something new, go for it. Also, internships don't last forever, so if it turns out you don't like the career area you're exploring, at least you'll find out now and not after you've spend several years preparing for it.

***

Going After Your Passion and Being Realistic

You've probably heard the phrase *Follow your passion*. Unfortunately, your passion at the moment may not directly line up with an internship. Sometimes you may just find a fit, and that's great when it happens.

Don't be discouraged if you can't find an internship that matches up exactly with your passion or dream. There might be something related to the area you're hoping for or some aspect of a career area that you never knew about. It can't hurt to widen your view and try it out!

Many young people at this point in their lives have dreams, and an internship can help them start on the road to achieving that dream or help them understand the reality of work in that field.

***

Alex

Alex is a senior at Central High. He is usually a quiet, average student and is liked by other students and teachers. Alex has no idea about what he wants to do after graduation.

When my guidance counselor met with me to plan for my senior year and asked me what I wanted to do after graduation, all I could say was, "I don't know." I don't think she was happy with this answer.

I finally told her my friends and I were really big on skateboarding. There are a couple of places we skateboard around town.

I thought that was the end of it, but then a couple of days later she called me in and asked me if I would be interested in doing an internship at a sports store that sold all kinds of sports equipment and also worked with some sports clubs and teams. I said, "Sure, why not." And besides, I bet my mom and dad would be happy I was doing something besides just hanging around.

Alex was lucky that his guidance counselor got him to talk about what really interested him.

She was then able to help him find an internship where he could be connected with skateboarding and also learn about other sports and sports clubs in the city. Alex probably knew he would not be the next National Skateboard Champion, but he was still able to find an internship that included some of his interest in skateboarding along with practical exploration of the wider field of sports-equipment sales and marketing.

Tip: Even if you can't find a site that exactly matches your dream career, dig deeper into related fields. If you want to be a musician and there's no recording studio or venue near you, perhaps there's another location that holds events and you could learn the business and management end of the music or production world. When it comes to eventually getting paid, you'll want to know how the business and management end works.

***

Using your school is a great way to find an internship that's right for you. There are probably many internships that you would like to do and some that you may not even have thought about.

If your school doesn't have an internship program, talk with your guidance counselor. She'll ask you some questions about your plans and what your interests are. Be honest. You might be surprised at some of the opportunities that are there for you.

You can also check out your school's career center. Don't just think this is for students who want to get into business. Your career center has a lot of information and may have an internship program.

Your guidance counselor or career center might suggest that you take an online career inventory. Do it. This will tell you about what you may like or dislike when thinking about your future. The results can point you in the right direction as you start making decisions about what you want to do or where you want to go.

Stretch Yourself

You may or may not have already have committed yourself to a field of study in college, or you think you're sure you know what you want to do after graduation. You may be asking, "Can an internship really help me at this point?" Again, the answer is a resounding *YES*!

***

Luis

Luis will graduate from East Community College this year. His major is Web Design and Development, and he has always thought that he would become a Web designer. He loves the technical-development work but has been thinking recently that he would like to get more involved with a business that works directly with clients in website design. He wants face-to-face contact with clients and not just work online or in a back office.

As part of my college program I needed to do an internship. The college partnered with some companies that had internships lined up for the students in Web design. But the work experience was just the development of the websites and learning coding and working on various technical aspects of Web design. I'm interested in that, but I also want to do more than just work online designing websites, so I decided to find my own internship.

I short-listed the companies in my city that I thought would be interested in my skills and that worked directly with clients. These were advertising agencies, consulting companies, and graphic-design companies. I e-mailed each to see if they would be interested in my skills and in offering me an internship. A week later I got a reply from City Net Design asking me to submit my résumé and call for an interview. So I did.

I hope this company is thinking about a paid internship.

Luis wasn't happy with the types of internships available for students in his program and decided to find one that would be more challenging. He was focused on his career and knew he needed experience in working face-to-face with clients in order to get the kind of job he wanted after graduation. He was willing to pass up a set internship to look for one that better met his goals and he was successful. He was also willing to do the work to find a better placement.

> ✒ **Tip:** Finding the internship that you'll enjoy and learn from takes some effort—and time. Even though some sites might be available, make sure you really want to be there before you commit to spending your time there. Your internship doesn't have to be a perfect fit, but it should at least hold some interest for you.

***

Need Help?

Sometimes finding the right internship may not be so straightforward even if you know what you want to do. You may start out with one plan in mind only to find that something holds more interest and challenge for you.

***

Jessica

Jessica thought she knew what she wanted. Throughout high school Jessica said that all she wanted to do was to be a police officer. Her dad was a detective, and she wanted to be one, too. After graduation Jessica enrolled in the criminal-justice program at Willington Community College. She was well on her way. And she did an internship with the county police department in her first year.

The best part of that internship for me was the time I spent training in cybercrime. I didn't even know there was such a thing. That's when I decided to change my major to cybersecurity. This was a big step for me, and my academic adviser helped me with the switch. I'm lucky that my college has a great program called the Homeland Security and Criminal Justice Institute.

Jessica's internship helped her decide on the part of law enforcement that really interested her. When she began her new program, she applied to do an internship in cybersecurity.

I really got a lot out of my first internship with the police depart-ment. It helped me to define what I want to do. It also showed me different aspects of law enforcement. I am so excited about doing an internship in cyber security. I know I have a lot to learn. I want to be sure that I show what I learned at my first internship on my résumé for my new internship in cybersecurity.

Sometimes you may find that your internship opens doors to other opportunities you might not have even thought of, and it may send you in a different direction. If you've done an internship, you may want to do another in a different field or a more challenging one in your own field. The experience you get in your internship will help you make the right choices going forward.

TIP: If you get a chance to do more than one internship . . . take it. What you learned at the first one can really help you at the second one. And maybe you'll get to explore a different career area or a different aspect of one you've experienced before.

***

Still Need Help?

If you aren't really sure what you want to do, you may need to take a few more steps before you get to the point where you can narrow down your search.

If you have no idea where you'd like to intern, perhaps trying a few interest inventories online will help you think about what you *do* like and what you *don't* like—and what you do and don't value about cer-tain work situations. That's a start.

If your school has interest inventories, take them. It could help you begin to think about what career areas you'd like to explore.

You might also want to go to the sites listed at the end of this chapter (EXTRA INFO 1A: Work Values Inventories, and EXTRA INFO 1B: Career Interest Inventories), which offer free inventories. Just remem-ber, the results of a single inventory do not mean that you're destined to follow the suggested career path forever. These are just informational to be used to get you thinking of possibilities.

Also, check out the list at the end of this chapter for some ideas (EXTRA INFO 1C: Ideas for Internships). This is a list of some internship sites where students across the country have interned. The list is not at all complete, but it can give you some ideas if you need something to get you thinking.

Your goal at this point is to decide where you would like to intern and to come up with a list of three or four possible locations to do that.

MORE TO THINK ABOUT

What About Pay?

This is an issue that can cause some students to not even consider an internship. Don't ignore an internship opportunity just because there is no pay involved. An internship is about more than money. It's about what you can learn and the skills you can acquire that will help you for the rest of your life. You could be passing up a chance to get so much more than a paycheck.

Many internships for students who have not yet graduated from college are not paid because they're considered to be mainly learning experiences. The intern is there to learn and grow. Many times interns get school credit instead of pay. Sometimes internships can be paid especially when the skills that the intern has contributes to the company or if the sponsoring company or organization has a formal internship program.

***

Luis
This may be the case with Luis.

> *I'm not sure this internship with City Net Design will be paid. But I think it should be. I know that some students in my program were able to get paid internships because they had solid Web design skills that would benefit the company. I hope this is the case for me. I am going make sure my résumé highlights my Web skills, and I'll ask about pay in my interview if they don't bring it up.*

Luis has taken on the challenge of selling his skills to show that he can contribute to the company while at the same time learning about working with clients.

> **Tip:** Not getting paid for work can really bother some people. But instead of pay, a lot of internship programs pay the student in the form of credit toward their school requirements. If you view an unpaid internship as a learning experience that will be with you as you move into the next phase of your life, you'll see that you're getting a lot out of it. Some older interns do get paid. Each situation is unique, and there are pros and cons to all of them.

***

Get Some Credit

Michelle, Alex, Luis, and Jessica will most likely get school credit for their internships because they're being done under the umbrella of the school or college. Schools or colleges award between one and three credits depending on the internship. Perhaps there are credits given for a separate internship course or certain projects in a class are waived if a student completes an internship. It is worth finding out what credit you can earn and what the requirements are.

Even though Luis found his own internship, the experience is part of his degree program. He will need to let his college know why he chose to find his own internship and what he expects to learn from his experience. Luis probably won't have any trouble getting the required credit for his internship.

Part-Time Work

What happens if you have a part-time job and want to gain internship credit for it? You may or may not be able to use your part-time job as an internship depending on your school or college.

The first thing to do is let your guidance counselor, academic adviser, teacher, or internship coordinator know that you want to use your work experience as internship experience. You'll also need to let your manager know that this is what you want to do.

Remember, an internship is more than just work. It's about you learning new skills in a planned and structured way. Your school may develop a plan with you so that you can do some additional projects and show how you've developed new skills.

Once you've agreed on the way forward with your school or college and your manager, you may get credit for your work. But be prepared to put in extra hours when you're not getting paid to do your internship project work.

Some students have been able to use their paid part-time work as an internship, but it is tricky. You need to do your groundwork, get the right people involved, and negotiate a workable plan.

WHAT'S NEXT?

You've decided that you want to do an internship and have taken the first steps by letting your school or college know that you're interested. As you start on your way you'll need to make sure your résumé shows what you've accomplished. And you'll need to get your thoughts organized so you have a story to tell about yourself when you go to that interview for your internship.

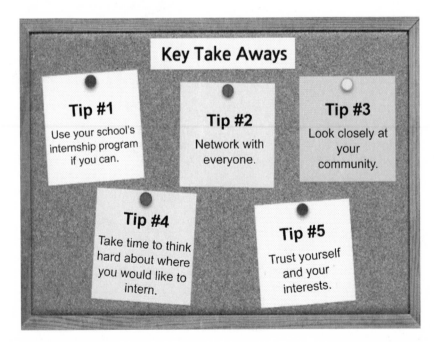

EXTRA INFO 1A: Work Values Inventories

Work Values Test (123Test.com)
http://www.123test.com/career-values-test/

Career Test (123Test.com)
http://www.123test.com/career-test/

Skills Inventory (University of Minnesota, Duluth)
http://www.d.umn.edu/kmc/student/loon/car/self/career_transfer_
survey.html

EXTRA INFO 1B: Career Inventories

O*NET Interest Profiler: My Next Move
http://www.mynextmove.org/explore/ip
Sponsored by the US Department of Labor: Employment and Training Administration, and developed by the National Center for O*NET Development

ISEEK Career Cluster Interest Survey
http://www.iseek.org/careers/clusterSurvey
Copyright 1999–2014, iSeek Solutions

EXTRA INFO 1C: Ideas for Internships

Interest Area	Possible Internship Sites
Agriculture, Food, and Natural Resources	animal caretaking (pet sitter, trainer, groomer), eco-tour company, farms, floral department, grocery store, florists, gardening center, humane organization, landscaper, conservation organization, parks and recreation site, government conservation department, environmental protection laboratory and department, fish and wildlife department, municipal recycling center, nursery, ranch, recreational ranch, veterinary practice, wildlife rescue and rehabilitation, zoo or animal park
Architecture and Construction	architecture firm, civil engineering firm, construction-material company, home-building/remodeling company, local government engineering department, local government planning board, local building inspection department
Arts, A/V Technology, and Communications	artisan, community cable station, cultural center, digital design company, film production company, graphic arts company, graphics and reproduction firm, interior decorator, local journal, local newspaper, local theater, multimedia production company, museum, historical site, news-photography agency, online magazine, painter, photographer, radio station, retail-store window display, television station
Business Management and Administration	charitable organization, environmental organization, HR employee-benefits office, local business or nonprofit administration department, service organization
Education and Training	aerobics class (instructor), after-school recreational center, boys and girls club, classroom, day-care center, fitness center (trainer), music and art school, nursery school, parent resource center, preschool, special education class, sports program
Finance	accounting firm, bank or credit union, local brokerage house, local insurance company or agency
Government and Public Administration	elected official's local office (local, state, national), local town office department, municipal service, recycling center
Health Science	dental office, health clinic, hospital (all departments), medical examiner's office, medical laboratory, medical office, medical records departments, occupational therapy center, optometrist, pharmacy, physical therapy practice, public health office, speech therapy center, yoga center, health and wellness center, gym

(Continued)

Interest Area	Possible Internship Sites
Hospitality and Tourism	active sports center, caterer, historical site, hotel and conference center, institution, local hotel or inn, tourism office, restaurant, travel agency
Human Services	food bank, senior center (meal service, medical-appointment assistant service, ride service), social services agency or organization
Information Technology	businesses with IT departments, computer-research consulting firm, information and research provider, library, local computer company, local government IT department
Law, Public Safety, Corrections, and Security	fire department, police department, sheriff's department, courts and court services, law office, emergency medical service
Manufacturing	local or regional manufacturing company
Retail/Wholesale Sales and Services	home-supply or building company, large department store, clothing shop, retail store or company, wholesale company
Marketing	advertising agency, business with marketing department, college or university Public Relations (PR) department, market research company, marketing company or department, media-buying agency, PR agency, publicity or PR firm
Science, Technology, Engineering, and Mathematics	business with research and development department, computer software engineering company, computer-support firm, database administration department, local engineering company, medical lab, network-administration department, renewable energy company or nonprofit
Transportation, Distribution, and Logistics	transportation-related business (aircraft maintenance firm, airport, aviation school, aviation supply company, auto-detailing company, auto glass repair company, service station, bicycle sales and repair, boat builder, boatyard or marina, district school-bus provider), distribution and logistics–related business (mail center, shipping company [UPS, FedEx], warehouse distribution center

Source: Adapted from "The 16 Career Clusters®," National Association of State Directors of Career Technical Education Consortium, Career Clusters.

❷

Things You Need to Have

It would be great if all you needed to do to get an internship were to make a phone call and set a date to begin. No such luck. There are a few things that you need to do to get to the starting line. These are things you'll use over and over again in the real world.

DO I REALLY NEED A RÉSUMÉ?

Yeah, you do need a résumé.

Having a résumé is a way to keep track of all your employment, activities, achievements, and skills in one place.

Going through the process and completing a résumé is an accomplishment itself. It helps you send a clear message to a potential internship sponsor or employer that you care enough about yourself and the internship process to put in the effort to produce a good résumé. It says you are serious about your internship and your future. A résumé helps you think about the things you've accomplished so far, and it can give you a new sense of confidence.

Getting Your Résumé in Shape

At the same time you're researching and deciding on a list of places you may want to intern, you're going to need to polish up your résumé or create one if you don't have it already.

Some internship programs only require an application, but if you begin now to build a résumé for yourself, you can keep updating it as you gain experience. If an application is required, you'll be able to reference your résumé for important dates and information. A résumé is portable, current, and looks professional. An application form that you fill out on site, by hand, may not turn out so well. It won't look as professional as having a résumé to include.

***

Alex
When Alex was in the guidance counselor's office picking up the information he needed before his interview for his internship, she happened to ask if he wanted her to review his résumé.

> *What résumé? I didn't think I needed a résumé. I thought I was just going to have to fill out an application. I didn't have any real work experience, but my guidance counselor helped me figure out things I hadn't even thought about . . . like the part-time jobs I do for my uncle and the school plays I worked on with the stage crew . . . and my entry into the Career Day Fair. I forgot all about that.*
>
> *I was afraid I'd have an empty sheet of paper with just my name on it. And then when I got to the interview, the guy who interviewed me asked me for my résumé for their files. Good thing I had one to give him.*

As Alex learned, it's good to talk with a guidance counselor or teacher to help with writing or updating your résumé. She can help you remember activities and work you may have forgotten about. And she can help you write up your experiences so they look good on a résumé. The whole process can seem like an impossible task at first, but it doesn't have to be.

 Tip: Have teachers and others review your résumé. A fresh set of eyes can catch what you might have missed.

***

About Résumés and Cover Letters

Your **résumé** is a document that itemizes your employment and experience history. Your **cover letter** (or cover e-mail) is written to highlight the qualifications you have for the position for which you are applying.

Résumé

If you have a résumé already, you can update it. If you're connected with a school that has faculty that can help you, talk with someone and update or build your resume.

There is no such thing as a perfect résumé and there are examples at the end of this chapter that may fit your needs. You just need to find a format that works for you. Don't stress over one format over another. It's the content that really matters.

Cover Letters

A cover letter (or cover e-mail) is a document that you send with your résumé to provide additional information about your skills and experience or to call attention to what makes you a good fit for the position for which you are applying.

It not only tells of your accomplishments but also reveals how effectively you can communicate.

Your cover letter (or cover e-mail) is your first impression. It's important to spend time composing a good one for every site to which you are applying. You will need to tailor each cover letter to each position because one size does not fit all when it comes to cover letters.

***

Michelle
Michelle had a hard time getting started on her résumé. This was the first time she had ever needed one, and she didn't know where to begin.

Since I had spent all my spare time taking care of my sisters, I really didn't have time to do any real work. The head of the career center pointed out that what I was doing was work and I wasn't giving myself enough credit for what I had done. He also asked me some questions, and I realized I had been doing volunteer work for several years and I also had really good grades.

Michelle thought unpaid work, volunteer experience, and academic accomplishments didn't have any importance in a résumé, but she soon realized these are the things that help interviewers see what type of person you are. They are the things you value and have accomplished in your current role of student.

Tip: Don't undervalue your academic achievements, volunteer and part-time work, and your extracurricular and non-school activities.

***

If You Need Help

There are links in EXTRA INFO 2A: Résumés and Cover Letters at the end of this chapter that deal with résumé writing, especially for students without a great deal of work experience.

Your school probably has teachers or administrators or someone else to assist with your résumé and point you in the right direction for additional help. Go to them and ask for their help.

Even if you've graduated or are no longer actively enrolled, some schools will offer their career- and internship-placement services to you. It can't hurt to ask. Some people pay big bucks for advice and information that you might be able to get just by having a connection to an educational institution.

Résumés that Michelle, Jessica, Luis, and Alex used for their internship interviews are included as examples at the end of this chapter in EXTRA INFO 2B: Student Résumé Examples.

TIPS ABOUT RÉSUMÉS, COVER LETTERS, COVER E-MAILS, REFERENCES, AND E-MAIL ADDRESSES

Check Details, and Think Ahead

- Check for spelling or grammar errors in your résumé, and try not to let the entire document get longer than a page. Get several other people to review it and point out edits.
- References. You must ask people if you can use their names as references on your résumé *before* you list them. No excuses. If you don't ask, you could be in for an unpleasant surprise.
- Keep your résumé on a flash drive or your phone, and keep it with you. You never can tell when you may need to print it or refer to it.

About E-mailing Résumés and Cover Letters

Chances are you may need to send your résumé and cover letter by e-mail, so you should plan for that situation. In EXTRA INFO 2A at the end of this chapter there is a link to information about formatting a résumé and cover letter for e-mailing.

Cover E-mails and Subject Lines

- Subject line. Don't leave this blank. Use something like *Internship Position—[Your Name]* or *Internship Application—[Your Name]*.
- Make the cover e-mail similar to your cover letter.
- Address the person the same way as your cover letter (e.g., *Dear Mr. Smith*).
- Close with *I look forward to hearing from you. Thank you for your consideration.*
  Sincerely,
  [Your Name]
- Keep the e-mail short as Luis did in his search for an internship.

Dear Ms. Brown:

   I am interested in obtaining an internship in which I can use my website-design skills directly with clients. If you have an internship position available, I would be happy to send my résumé to you.

E-mail Addresses

Often students say, "I really don't want to change my e-mail address just to look for an internship. That seems like such a hassle. Can't I just use the one I've been using forever?" The answer is always the same— "It depends." If your E-mail address begins with "luvbug" or "treehugger," you need to change it. Seriously. Would *you* take luvbug@e-mail.net as an intern?

E-mail Signatures

"I don't see what's wrong with smiley faces on the screen! Do I have to get rid of them?" That was a real question. And, yeah, you do need to get rid of them . . . *right away*. Get all quotations, photos, or sayings off your automated e-mail signature. They don't say "serious" or "professional."

Or just set up another e-mail address that you can use professionally going forward. Keeping professional and private lives separate is a good practice anyway. It can't hurt to start now.

A Note

Some businesses and organizations may specify that they don't open e-mail attachments. If so, both your cover letter and résumé will have to be included in the body of the e-mail. Make sure to space them apart to make it easier to distinguish each document. There is a link in the EXTRA INFO 2A at the end of this chapter where you can learn about making sure documents such as résumés are in the correct format for e-mailing or attaching to e-mails.

THE ELEVATOR SPEECH/PITCH

What do you mean *elevator speech*? Why would I make a speech in an elevator?

The term comes from the time it takes to complete a normal elevator ride from the top to the bottom floor. It is a mini speech that's useful any time you need to quickly explain who you are, what knowledge and skills you have, and what goals you're working toward.

Why Would I Need One?

Your elevator speech is your quick, personal selling speech. It is meant to tell someone who you are, what you want (goals), and what you have to offer (enthusiasm, interest, any experience). It can be used when you find yourself riding in an elevator unexpectedly with the head of the company, or when you end up standing beside someone you've been hoping to talk with, or any other situation where you may be near enough to have a brief conversation with someone who can help you advance your goals. An elevator speech can also serve as the foundation for cover letters, e-mail introductions, meeting employers at career fairs, and other more informal social settings.

You might want to memorize the key points of your elevator speech so that you don't get nervous and bumble around and ramble on at a key time. Some people even memorize the whole speech, but that can make the delivery seem stiff and too formal. Your goal should be to have confidence and deliver your points while looking at the other person with a genuine expression of interest.

How to Develop an Elevator Speech

Your elevator speech should help you make a good first impression and include the following five pieces of information:

1. Who you are, plus a credential/relationship. Include your name and something that sets you apart from others (recent graduate/ current student at _____, athlete, awards winner, etc.) and establishes a relationship (graduate of same school, from the same home town, parents or relative know each other, have known about their business since you were young, etc.).

***

Jessica
Jessica had a very good credential to offer at the beginning of her elevator speech:

It's a pleasure to meet you. I'm Jessica Davison, and I'm currently a student in criminal-justice studies at the community college. After my first semester there, I have decided to concentrate on cybercrime. I'll be refocusing my major for the summer term so I can begin the Homeland Security and Criminal Justice Institute program for cybercrime, and I've already taken a course in computer forensics.

In the meantime, I am hoping to learn more about the computer-programming side of this career area. I know this is a constantly changing field and it's important to keep up with new developments.

An internship with a computer-security company would help me see firsthand how companies are affected by cybercrime and how security companies are working to fight back. I feel that the courses I have already taken plus my current computer skills would help me gain a great deal of experience, information, and insight into the field I plan to enter.

Jessica covered a lot in one short speech, and she was direct about her change of major and her excitement about that decision.

> **Tip:** Try to mention at least one accomplishment or connection with the person or field you're pursuing in your elevator speech. It will help the person you're talking with see you as someone who is serious, not someone who is just looking around.

***

2. Your specific goal/internship interest. Including this will allow that person to help you or possibly connect you to someone else who can. (*I'm hoping to arrange an internship that will help me explore the various aspects/departments/divisions of a particular career; seeking an internship that will permit me to apply the skills learned in specific school courses to a specific job sector; hoping to obtain an internship to learn more about a particular career and how my skills and long-time interest might be a match.*)

3. How you've demonstrated your interest. Demonstrate your interest and experience in the field with examples of things you've already completed. Don't just say, "I have always wanted to work with animals." Give more details such as, "I have worked two summers with the local animal-rescue league and have shadowed the town's animal control officers."

***

Alex

Although Alex has had no actual experience in business, his interest in sports and his passion for skateboarding and ability to repair and assemble equipment helps in making his case.

Hello. I'm Alex. Alex Boyd. I'm looking for an internship for next semester. My guidance counselor suggested I do an internship in something related to sports because I am really interested in sports, especially skateboarding. I'm really good with fixing sports equipment and assembling things, too. And I'm also really good with computers.

I'll be graduating in June, and it's time for me to figure out if I want to go to work or go to college or maybe both. So, if you have an internship opening, I would be interested in talking to you about it.

Alex missed mentioning the work he did for his uncle, but he does manage to talk about his passion for sports and his skills in working with sports equipment.

> **Tip:** Don't sell yourself short. If you've done something or accomplished something, mention it. It's not bragging. It's letting someone know you a little better.

***

4. Why you're qualified. Demonstrate your qualifications by sharing leadership and work experience, achievements, expertise, skills, and strengths.

***

Luis

Luis has special skills and has had experience using them, which should be of interest to companies looking for an intern in this area.

Hi. My name is Luis Belen, and I am a second-year student at East Community College, majoring in Web design and development with a focus on website design and maintenance. I have just completed a new website for the Adams Settlement House and am currently working on a website for a relative's crafts business.

During my studies at the college I've been able to experience many different aspects of the graphic-design areas, and I find that what I like best is working directly with clients and helping them through the steps necessary to end up with the website they envision. I realize that Web design is a field that changes quickly, and that's why I would like to spend some time in an Internet-design company interning with people who build and design websites for a living.

I think my experience and fresh eye might be of value to a company, and I would be able to learn a great deal.

Luis is able to mention his experience in design and is clear about his goal of working with clients.

> **Tip:** If you have experience or skills in the area you're pursuing, that's a bonus. Let people know that. Now is not the time to hold back.

***

5. A question or request for assistance. Consider giving the person two options for ways they might help. For example, "If your company/office offers internships, I would appreciate the name of the person in charge of that program." Or, "Perhaps I could meet with you in person to find out more about your organization and opportunities in the marketing profession."

> TIP: Make sure you have a copy of your résumé in a business envelope, on a flash drive or on your phone in case someone asks for it.

***

Michelle

Michelle's request is for an opportunity for career exploration, and her elevator speech reveals that directly.

Hello. My name is Michelle Reddington, and I am a senior at Centertown High School this year. I'll be graduating in June, and I'm hoping to obtain an internship for my last semester. My guidance counselor, Ms. Jones, suggested I explore interning somewhere that would give me an opportunity to work with a team of people on projects, as I've enjoyed those types of activities all through school.

Although I've had a great deal of experience working with children, I would like to learn more about other careers that involve working closely with others to accomplish things.

I noticed that this hotel has worked with interns in the past, and Ms. Jones described some of the projects former interns have worked on. The work you do here seems quite interesting, so I decided to pursue an internship with this company.

Michelle is able to show her enthusiasm to try something new and that she has enjoyed working with a team before.

> TIP: Let the person you're talking with know that you're looking for an actual internship . . . not just to talk about the career area. That would be an informational interview and something totally different. If you aren't clear, they may not understand that you actually want something.

***

Now Write Your Own Speech

It's time to put together your own elevator speech. Perhaps you already have one. But if not, use this template to get started.

Hello, my name is _____, and I am completing a _____ degree/certificate in _____ at _____ with a minor in _____. **OR** I am a recent graduate of _____. **OR** I am currently enrolled as a student at _____.

I am interested in a career in [or position as a] _____ in the _____ field [industry].

I have been involved in _____ and developed skills in _____. I have also had an internship position [employment] as a _____ with _____ and discovered that I really enjoy _____.

Could you tell me more about internship opportunities at _____? **OR** I would appreciate an opportunity to talk with you about a possible internship position in your _____ department. **OR** Perhaps you can direct me to the person I need to speak with about an internship at [company name].

Once you're happy with your speech, read it over and over. Some people memorize it, and that's fine if you can deliver it without sounding stiff and robotic. The best thing to do is be very familiar with the points you want to make and memorize those.

ALL THIS PAPERWORK!

Résumés. Cover letters. Cover e-mails. Elevator speeches. It seems like a lot of hoops to jump through just to get an internship. But these are the things that are needed in the world outside of school. People get a sense of what kind of person you are by looking at these documents.

Most sponsors are used to working with young adults and understand that you don't have the experience of someone older who has been working for a while. But they still like to see that you've made the effort and have begun to understand that looking for an internship is practice for one day looking for a job. The sponsors who are happy to work with interns often say they wish they had had an opportunity to intern when they were in school and that's one of the reasons why they're happy to spend time helping and mentoring young adults on their way to adulthood.

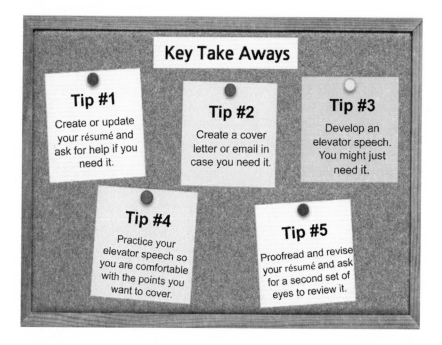

EXTRA INFO 2A: Résumés and Cover Letters

Resources for Résumés and Cover Letters
The sites listed here will give you information on how to get started on writing a résumé and how to improve an existing one. There are also links to sample résumés and formats to help you. Your school may have its own suggested format, or you may find books or other resources online. Use whatever works best for you.

Cover letters are just as important as résumés, but you can't write the letter until you decide which internship you want to apply for. Don't wait to do the résumé and cover letter together.

Guides to writing Résumés
Teen Résumé Guide
https://www.cityofboston.gov/images_documents/Teen_Résumé_Guide_tcm3-31427.pdf

Damn Good Résumé Guide—free résumé tips, résumé samples, and résumé help
http://damngood.com

The Résumé Workbook for High School Students
http://damngood.com/workbooks/highschool.pdf

Monroe Community College Guide
http://www.monroecc.edu/depts/careercenter/stuserv/résumécomposing.htm

Résumé Examples
http://jobsearch.about.com/od/samplerésumé1/a/high-school-résumé-examples.htm

Guides to Writing Cover Letters or Cover E-mails
Susan Ireland's Résumé Site—cover letters
http://susanireland.com/letter/how-to/
http://susanireland.com/good-cover-letter-samples/

Jobstar Central—About Cover Letters
http://jobstar.org/tools/résumé/cletters.php

Making Sure Your Résumé Is Good to Go as an Attachment
Check out this site to make sure your résumé will appear correctly if you send it as an e-mail attachment.
http://susanireland.com/job-lounge/what-résumé-format-is-best-for-email-attachment/

EXTRA INFO 2B: Student Résumé Examples

Michelle Reddington

6 Pine Street, Centertown, CA
Home 555.555.5555
Cell: 222.222.2222
mredddington@email.com

EDUCATION: Centertown High School. Expected graduation — June (date)

WORK EXPERIENCE: Child Care   (date) — Present

- Provide child care for several families weekends and during school vacations
- Provide childcare and homework help for siblings early mornings and after school daily

VOLUNTEER EXPERIENCE

- Big Brother / Big Sisters — Homework Helper
- Centertown Public Library
- High School fundraising team to aid the homeless food
- Town food pantry, collecting, stocking, outreach

ACHIEVEMENTS

- National Honor Society: (date)— Present
- Academic Honor Roll: (date) — Present
- Student Government , Secretary (date — Present)

INTERESTS / ACTIVITIES

- Member of Centertown High School Cross Country Team
- Year Book Production Committee
- Girl Scouts

COMPUTER SKILLS   Proficient with

- Microsoft Word, Excel, and PowerPoint
- Online Database Research, and
- Basic Wix Web Design.

References:

Mr. Seth Smith, English Teacher
Centertown High School
(Work) 555.555.5555
(Home)222.222.2222
email: ssmith1@email.com

Ms. M.L. Jones, Librarian
Centertown Public Library
(Work) 555.555.5555
(Home)222.222.2222
email: mljones@email.com

Alex Boyd
10 Cedar Street, Place, FL 12345
Home: 555.555.5555
Cell: 566.486.2222
E-mail: aboyd@email.net

EDUCATION   Central High School, Place, FL
Graduation Anticipated (Date)

WORK EXPERIENCE

Franklin Auto Service, Place, FL (Date) to Present

- Assist family business to provide detailing service to customer's automobiles

- Create and distribute 200 flyers about Detailing service

- Help collate invoices for monthly billing and enter payments into Quicken software

Pet Sitter (Date) - Present

- Provide pet sitting services including dog walking, feeding and mail pick up to neighborhood homes

INTERESTS / ACTIVITIES

- Member of Central High School Drama Club – Stage Crew
- Designed and built skateboard for Career and Technology Fair

COMPUTER SKILLS
  • Proficient with Microsoft Word, Excel, Internet, Social Media, Quicken

Reference:

Mr. James Wyatt, CTE Teacher
Central High School
home: 555.555.5555
cell: 566.486.2222
E-mail: jwyatt@email.net

Jessica Davison

6 Elm Avenue
Willington, MD 12345
766.444.4444   jdavison1234@email.com

EDUCATION

Willington County Community College — Criminal Justice Program. Currently enrolled.
Relevant Courses: Introduction to the Criminal Justice System; Criminal Law; Overview of
Cybercrime; Computer Forensics I

Willington High School, Willington, MD - High School Diploma (Date)

WORK EXPERIENCE

Willington Police Department – Intern (Dates)
- Participated in 8 week training for local police departments in Department of Justice
  Cybercrimes Training
- Participated in cases involving detective and forensic units, court appearances, case follow-up
- Participated in sit-alongs, ride-alongs with detectives and patrolmen

Super Snacks – Scooper (Dates)
- Provided friendly customer service in small family ice-cream/organic snack store
- Handled cash and credit card transactions and balanced out register nightly
- Monitored inventory ad assisted with reordering inventory

Sam's Subs – Counter (Dates)
- Restocked condiments, napkins and maintained a clean counter.
- Provided great customer service for walk-in customers on each shift.
- Operated cash register, POS, and frequent guest card system.

COMPUTER SKILLS Proficient with
- Microsoft Word, Excel, and PowerPoint
- Internet Research, online database research
- Installing/uninstalling computer software
- Checking computers for virus and other malware.

VOLUNTEER EXPERIENCE
- Willington Toys for Tots Drive – Head of area collection team past four years
- Police Athletic League – Active with all summer activities for past three years
- Library -Homework Helpers Reading Program –past two years

INTERESTS
Community Basketball Team; Race for the Cure - Helped with organization and set up and ran with
local Police Athletic League (PAL) team.

References

Captain Carolyn Smith	Sergeant Jack McDell, PAL	Marissa Kennely, Owner
Willington Police Department	Coordinator	Super Snacks
555-555-5555	Willington Police Department	444-444-44
	555-555-5555	

luis belen

295 Main Avenue   • East, IL • 12345
CELL (555) 123-7654 • **E-MAIL** lbelen@email.com

EDUCATION	**East Community College,** East Campus, East IL Anticipate **AS degree**, Web Design, June (date) Honor roll each quarter
	East High School, East, IL Graduated (date) Yearbook Committee, Intramural Volleyball
WORK EXPERIENCE	**Panera** - September (date) - Present • Lead Set-up team to organize coffee and soft drinks service area for each shift
	McDonalds (Dates) • Customer Service order taking and filling
	ABC Supermarket – Night Shift (Dates) • Team member responsible for inventory and shelf stacking

COMPUTER SKILLS

• Photoshop	• Microsoft Word
• Muse	• Power Point
	• Excel

VOLUNTEER EXPERIENCE

Tutor, Adams Settlement House (dates)
• Helped elementary school students with homework assignments
• Served snacks and helped students with clean up
• Participated in afterschool recreation activities

Soup Kitchen Server, Adams Settlement House (dates)
• Served holiday meals to homeless and other less fortunate community members
• Helped with set up and clean up

References:

Ms. Gloria Markham, Academic Advisor East Community College Work: 555-543-6543 Gmarkham@email.edu	Mr. Ben White, Manager Panera Work: 555-543-6543 bwhite1@gmail.com

❸

Get Ready for the Interview

You've decided to do an internship and have found some potential internship sites through your school or college or on your own. You've got your résumé together and have prepared your elevator speech. Now it's time to think about getting the internship you want.

SETTING UP YOUR INTERVIEW

Most companies will want to meet you before they agree to offer you an internship. And it probably will be your responsibility to set up that meeting.

If you've contact information, call or e-mail (if you can, find a direct e-mail address for the person you need to contact). The person you're contacting will probably be expecting your call or e-mail if you're part of your school's or college's internship program.

Ask the person if he would like you to send a résumé or complete an application before the interview. Agree on a time and place for the interview, and write down the information so you don't forget.

Remember, you're calling to set up a date and time for your interview, so have your calendar handy.

Sometimes things can get confused in e-mails and phone calls. So send a note or e-mail thanking the person and confirming that you'll be seeing him on the date and time you agreed.

Now that you have the time and date for your interview, you'll need to prepare.

GET READY FOR WHAT COMPANIES
AND ORGANIZATIONS WANT

You may be wondering what the interview will be like. You may also be wondering what kind of questions you'll be asked. Take the time before your interview to look at some of the things that are important to organizations and what you may be asked.

Skills and Attitudes that Matter

Most companies and organizations are clear about what they're looking for when they interview someone for an internship. The company wants to know if you'll interact effectively with coworkers and customers. They want to know if you'll fit into their culture—"how things are done around here."

And so the interviewer will be looking for the skills and attitudes that tell her that you'll be a good fit into the organization's culture. These skills are often referred to as *soft skills* or *life skills*. One writer calls them *survival skills*. Whatever they're called, how you show these skills and attitudes in your interview is all-important.

Organizations want you to have:

- **A positive attitude.** Do you have a can-do attitude? Can you talk about a time when you got something done against all odds? Are you willing to try something new? Are you enthusiastic about wanting an internship?
- **A good work ethic.** Can you show that you show up on time for the things you have to do? Do you complete your work on time? Can you show that you keep your promises? Can you talk about a project that you completed?
- **Good communication skills.** Do you answer the interviewer's questions with more than a *yes* or *no*? Are your answers clearly thought out? Do you ask questions about the company and the internship?
- **Teamwork skills.** Can you talk about working with others? Can you talk about being part of a team (a sports team, project team, band, theater group, or any team or group you participated in)? Can you show that you've listened to others' ideas?

Organizations know that most students who apply for an internship may not have had any work experience. Don't be put off by lack of experience. They're just trying to figure out if you'll get along with others and fit into their culture.

First Impressions Will Matter

Your interview will be the time that the interviewer will get to know a little about you. But there is another time that the interviewer will start to form an impression of you. The first time your interviewer sees you, she will start to form that all-important first impression of you. Whether she sees you sitting in a waiting room, standing at the reception desk, walking down the hall, or entering her office, the way you look and act will begin to form a picture of who you are.

So make sure you look and act like an intern and not a student.

- Dress like you mean it. Looking professional is part of the deal, so, please, no jeans, no hats, no gum, and no candy.
- Put your phone away. Checking messages or listening to your playlist while you're waiting for the interview to start does not get you in the right mood. Pay attention to where you are. You're not killing time but are preparing for an interview.
- Rushing to your interview will make you hot and sweaty. Find out where your interview will be, and know how to get there.
- Don't sit like a slob. Remember, body language says a lot about you.
- You're in a business environment, so walk with confidence.

***

Alex

When Alex's guidance counselor met with him to help him set up his interview at Southeastern Sports, she said there were some other things she wanted to talk with him about.

After we set up my interview, my guidance counselor asked me if I always wore jeans and T-shirts to school. Well, yeah, that's what

I like. She then asked me if I had other kinds of pants and shirts. And I thought, What is she getting at? I said I had khakis and other shirts, like with a collar. She said that it was important to look like an intern when I go to the interview and not like a student. And then she asked me what I thought I should wear. Oh, now I got it. I should wear khakis and not a T-shirt because it would make me look more professional. I guess this is what I would need to wear if I get the internship.

Alex had probably never even thought about wearing something other than jeans and T-shirts until his guidance counselor raised the subject. But he immediately realized that he had to look more like an intern rather than a student when he went to his interview.

***

When you're arranging your interview, you might ask what the dress code is for the organizations. Be careful of the answer "business casual." This does not mean that anything goes. It does not mean that you can wear what you might wear to the beach or when hanging out with friends. You need to look neat and businesslike.

The way you look at your interview is important. Don't be the intern who shows up in a miniskirt and stiletto heels. Or the one who shows up in shorts and a T-shirt.

You don't want to be remembered as the intern who didn't know how to dress.

Tip: Take the time when you're preparing for your interview to think about how you come across to others. Make the changes that are needed.

GET READY FOR YOUR INTERVIEW QUESTIONS

You already have a lot of information about yourself that will help you in your interview. Your résumé has helped you pull together facts about yourself. Writing your elevator speech has made you think about who you are and what you want. Knowing what skills and attitudes an organization is interested in gives you a framework for how you want to present yourself. And if you're honest with yourself, a close look at your "student" appearance will show you how you might want to change some things to make that good first impression.

How can you use what you know and have discovered about yourself to answer questions in your interview?

Sometimes students who go to an interview for an internship have never been interviewed for anything before. And they're afraid that they won't have the answers to the interviewer's questions. But remember, the interview is not a test. It is a time for the interviewer to get to know you a little.

But What if I'm Shy?

Some students say that they don't do well in an interview situation because they're shy. They seem to believe that those students who are naturally talkative and outgoing will always succeed in an interview. Most interviewers know the difference between those individuals who are shy (or, in personality terms, introverted) and those who are outgoing (or extroverted). They know that being an extrovert, for example, will not automatically lead to being good at a job.

There are some real personality differences between introverts and extroverts.

Introverts

- Like to think things out before talking
- Can be quiet in meetings
- Like to concentrate on a few tasks at a time and
- Are more likely to consider things before acting.

Extroverts

- Will often think things out by talking them through
- Like to contribute in group meetings
- Like a variety of tasks and
- Can be impulsive.

The best organizations and teams need a mix of introverts and extroverts, and interviewers are very aware of this. So if you're shy, don't be afraid of the interview. If you're prepared and are able to show your strengths, you'll be fine.

Make a Strong Statement

Most companies and organizations will use the interview to start a conversation with you. They'll want to know more about you than what they have already read on your résumé. Usually the interviewer will start with some general questions.

She'll usually ask some questions that will give you a chance to talk about yourself.

***

Michelle

Michelle prepared for her interview at a local conference center hotel by reviewing her résumé and elevator speech so she would be ready to answer the question, "Can you tell me some things about yourself?"

Michelle planned to say:

> *I am a senior at Centertown High. I have finished most of my classes that I need for graduation and want to find an internship that will give me work experience and one where I can work with people.*
>
> *I participate in student government and am active in the school's fundraising for the homeless and the food pantry in my community. I also volunteer at the Boys and Girls Club where I help with homework for the kids in an elementary school.*
>
> *My mom is a single mom who has really worked hard to make sure my sisters and I have what we need. I know firsthand how families sometimes struggle to make sure that the kids have what they need. I think it's important to give back to your community.*

When Michelle practiced her answer, she forgot to include that she is an honor student and is in the honor society. Even though Michelle put these facts on her résumé, she missed the opportunity to highlight her achievements.

> **TIP:** If you get nervous in the real interview, you may forget to mention something that's important. Don't worry. Stay calm, and wait for the next question.

***

***

Luis

Luis wanted to highlight his experience in Web design and his team-work experience as he prepares to interview for an internship with a net-design company. He wanted to show his experience as he thought through his positive answer to the question, "Can you tell me why you want this internship?"

I will be getting my associate's degree at the end of this semester at East Community College. My major is in Web Design and Develop-ment, and I have used a number of graphics-design and animation programs.

I want to find an internship where I can use my technical skills in the real world. And I would like to work on a project with the end user so that I can see how the programs are actually used in the real world.

Most of my work experience has been in teams, which I really enjoy. I like the fact that I would be working on a client team in this internship. I also like the fact that my skills and technical knowledge would contribute to a project of importance to your clients.

In his planned response, Luis emphasizes his technical skills in Web design and development, something he said he wanted to do in his interview. He also indicates that he wants to work with clients and show that he has teamwork experience.

> **TIP:** Take the time to know who you are and what you want to do and to learn so you can answer any question about yourself.

***

***

Alex

Alex, too, prepared to answer the question, "Why do you want this internship?" as he got ready for his interview with a sports retailer.

> *I will graduate from Central High this June, and my guidance counselor asked me what I wanted to do. I wasn't sure, because I've never had a "real job." But when she told me about an internship in a sports store that sold sports equipment and got involved with sports programs, I thought I would like that.*
>
> *I'm really a big skateboarder, and I would like to do something with skateboarding when I graduate. But I don't know what that could be. So I guess this internship could show me what I could do. And it would be really great to see all the new skateboard designs and lots of other sports equipment.*

Alex's answer certainly isn't the best answer, but he is being honest and enthusiastic about skateboarding. If he had taken the time to learn more about the internship, the store, and what he could bring to the internship, he would have a better answer. Alex also forgets to highlight his work in his uncle's business. This information could be of interest to the interviewer.

 TIP: Don't forget that working for your family in their business can be great experience; so talk about it.

***

IMPORTANT INTERVIEW QUESTIONS

While using some general questions to break the ice, organizations today want to know how aware students are about the skills and attitudes needed to be a successful intern. The organization has defined precisely what kind of attitudes the interviewer will be looking for in these areas. To find this out, the interviewer will ask some specific questions that focus on those areas that are important.

Now is the time, before your interview, to think about what you might say. It's not good enough to fly by the seat of your pants as you answer these questions. The interviewer will know that you're not prepared. So look at these important areas and questions and see what the interviewer is looking for so you'll have good answers at your interview.

Key to Your Interview Success

Three areas are particularly important to most organizations:

- Work ethic
- Teamwork
- Communication

You've probably been lectured about your work ethic and your communication by parents, teachers, and everyone else. We know you've heard, "You have to work harder" or have been asked to "Tell me what is going on." And teamwork, you've been told, is good.

Now is the time to find out how organizations define these terms and what questions interviewers might ask you.

Work Ethic

This is the one area that is positively connected to success in your role as an intern. Generally having a good work ethic means that you consistently show up on time, meet any deadline, and get the job done. Specifically, an organization might define it as having a can-do outlook and a desire to succeed and is shown by:

- Accepting responsibility for your own work
- Completing work or activities on time
- Trying to do every activity "right the first time"
- Asking questions if you're not clear about what has to be done and
- Managing your own time to complete a task or activity.

Think about how you might prepare to give examples to answer the following questions:

- Can you tell me about a time when you had to set yourself an ambitious goal and what did you do to try to achieve it?
- Can you describe a time when you had to set priorities to meet a deadline?

> **Tip:** Use the real experiences you've had in school or college or at work to show how you met a deadline or set an ambitious goal. Be sure to mention what you learned from the experience.

Teamwork

Teamwork is important in most organizations. As an intern you'll find that you are part of a group or team. You'll not be on your own. Companies want to know that you can work with others, that you're aware of how teams work together, and that you're able to listen to others.

Good teamwork is showing a willingness to work with others and an understanding of your own contribution to team success.

An interviewer will want to know if you can give examples of working in a team as shown by:

- Understanding your own team role
- Giving information to others
- Treating individual team members the way they want to be treated
- Showing a willingness to help others and
- Showing an awareness of how your own actions impact on the team.

You might be asked:

- Can you tell me about a time you were part of a team? This may be a project team, sports team, a band or a group of friends who wanted to achieve the same goal. What did you learn from this experience?

> **Tip:** Talk positively about the real teams or groups you've been in. Give examples of how you shared information with others or helped out another team member.

This is the time, before the real interview, to think about how you might answer these questions.

While these may not be the specific questions you'll be asked, if you plan how to answer them you'll be able to show your work ethic and talk about your teamwork.

Communication

Good communication skills are vital for every person in an organization. While this is the one skill the interviewer will be looking for from the moment she greets you, the company will have specific communication skills it will want to see.

Your interviewer will notice if you're listening to your music or messaging while waiting or if you're slouching in your seat. Remember, first impressions matter. And your body language is all part of your communication.

Your interviewer might not ask you specific questions about how you communicate, but she will be listening to how you answer the questions in the interview.

Good communication means that an individual communicates clearly and to the point and can be shown to be:

- Speaking clearly
- Asking questions for information
- Listening to others
- Showing enthusiasm and
- Making positive statements about themself and others.

Your interviewer will want to know how well you communicate. She will be listening to the words you say and your tone. Now is the time to think about how you come across to others. Do you listen to them? Are you positive in the things you say about yourself and others? Can you talk enthusiastically about the things you do?

Remember, your interviewer will be listening to all that you say.

Tip: Show that you're enthusiastic in your interview by asking questions about the internship and organizations. Prepare those questions before your interview day.

WHEN IT'S YOUR TURN

Before the interviewer ends the interview, she will probably ask you if you have any questions. When you began looking for an internship, either through your school or college or on your own, you most likely short-listed some companies or organizations of interest to you. Now is the time to do more research by finding the organization's website, talking to people who know something about the organization or industry, and finding any articles by doing a Google search.

Formulate at least two questions you can ask at the end of your interview that will show you're interested in the company and the internship. If you have specific questions about the role, be sure you ask them. But keep some questions in reserve. The interviewer will want to know that you're interested, and asking relevant questions is your way of showing that you are.

You might want to ask the interviewer some of the following questions:

- What would be the hours of my internship?
- Will I have to be here weekends? (especially true for Michelle's and Alex's internships)
- What would my duties be as an intern?
- Are there other interns working here?
- Who would be my supervisor?
- Will I be given any training?

Most organizations have a website. Be sure you check it out before you go for your interview so you can ask some questions that are specific to the organization.

Practice, Practice, Practice

You don't need to have had work experience to answer any of the questions an interviewer might ask. But you do need to be prepared. Think through your answers to the questions you may get. Take the time. This will be the most important time you'll spend to get your internship.

Better yet, write out your answers, leave them for a day or two, and then reread them and make them better. When you get to your answers, you'll feel confident that you're ready for any question.

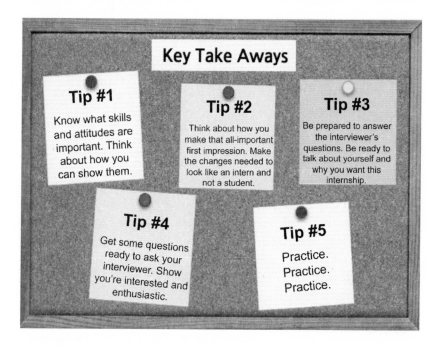

❹

Interview like a Pro

You prepared for the interview, and now it's time for the real thing.

You might be nervous about all the questions that you'll be asked that you might not have an answer to. Just stay calm, because you *are* prepared.

Remember, an interview is not a test. It's the time for the interviewer to start to get to know you.

You may be wondering who will do the interview and what the interview will be like.

There is no one way to interview a prospective employee or intern. Each company or organization has its own style. Most companies do one-to-one interviews, but some have two or more individuals interviewing the candidate at the same time. For your internship you most likely will have a one-to-one interview.

However, the person interviewing you could be the company owner or boss or a human-resources professional or the person who will be your supervisor or manager in your internship.

No matter who the person is, she will want to get to know you and see if you have what it takes to be a successful intern. And no matter who the interviewer is, she will know if you came prepared or are just winging it.

THE DAY OF YOUR INTERVIEW

You've thought about how you would answer possible questions, thought of some questions you want to ask, and checked that you'll make a good first impression. Now you're ready for your interview.

Remember:

- Arrive fifteen minutes early. Know where you're going so there is no rushing.
- No jeans, no gum, no candy, no hat. You're an intern, not a student.
- Dress professionally. You're not the intern who doesn't know how to dress for business.
- Go really light on cologne or perfume. You may be in a small room for your interview, and your interviewer may be allergic to some scents.
- Turn your phone off, and put it away. Your messages and music can wait.
- Put your water bottle away.
- Take a deep breath, and relax.

When you meet your interviewer, if you're sitting, stand up and greet her. Give your interviewer a firm handshake, and say something like "Thank you so much for taking the time to talk with me. I really appreciate it."

Your interview will start off with some polite conversation such as, "Did you have a hard time finding us?" or perhaps a comment about the weather. Remember, you're already making a first impression by how you look and what you say.

Before the formal interview starts, you may be offered a glass of water. Take it, as water will help soothe your throat if it gets dry.

What will the interviewer be thinking?

Even before the interview starts, your interviewer is already thinking:

- Do I like the way this person looks? Does he look more like a student than an intern?
- Is he polite?
- Does he have a firm handshake?
- Does he seem enthusiastic about being here?
- Does he make eye contact?

When the formal part of the interview starts, the interviewer will most likely have a list of specific things she wants to see. If you're asked some general questions—like, "Tell me about yourself" or "Why are you interested in interning with us?"—your interviewer will want to know whether:

- You speak clearly or mumble
- You make and keep eye contact
- You sound enthusiastic when answering questions
- You smile when appropriate and
- You're prepared to talk about yourself and why you want the internship.

Remember, this part of an interview is usually the start of the conversation that will allow the interviewer to get to know you.

Now the interviewer might switch to more specific questions. And here she will be looking for examples that make your points and to see if you listen to the question. She will want to hear a clear and concise answer.

HOW TO ANSWER THOSE IMPORTANT INTERVIEW QUESTIONS

The interviewer might say, "I'm going to ask you some questions and would like you to give examples in your answer. I'll be taking some notes so I can remember what you say."

Work Ethic

***

Michelle

At her interview Michelle was asked about her work ethic with the question, Can you *describe a time when you had to meet a deadline? This could be in a job you had or in completing a project in school. What did you do? Did you meet the deadline?*

Well, I had this project in school. It was on the First World War, and I had only four weeks to complete it. I wasn't sure of what

I had to cover, so I went to see my history teacher to get some more information.

We decided that I should focus on the impact the war had had on the American soldiers at the time. I knew I had to use a number of different sources to find information. So I made a chart of the various sources, like the textbook and other books, any letters or accounts of the war by soldiers, and the Internet. I knew I wanted to focus on the letters and writings of the soldiers who were there, but I had only a few weeks to get the information. So I found some books in the library and used the Internet to find some other writings and got a number of different accounts of how the war affected the soldiers. I was able to write the paper using my sources and get it in on time. But it was a tough subject. Someday I would like to read more of what the soldiers wrote, especially the poems.

Having a good work ethic means that you have a can-do outlook and a desire to succeed and that you're able to meet deadlines.

Michelle's interviewer wants to know if Michelle has a good work ethic.

Michelle showed that she:

- Handed in her project on time
- Worked to meet the deadline
- Made a chart of what needed to get done
- Took on an individual project and completed it and
- Asked her teacher for clarification.

Michelle's interviewer was looking for an example of how she met a deadline. Michelle was prepared, so was able to use an example of a school project. Michelle's answer was about an individual school assignment that she needed to complete using a variety of sources. She showed that she organized her work by making a chart of her sources, she asked her teacher for clarification of the assignment, and she met her time commitments.

> ✐ **Tip:** Don't worry if you may not have had any work experience. You can answer questions using your school or college experience.

***

***

Alex

Alex, who is also a senior in high school, was also asked to give an example about meeting a deadline in his interview at Southeastern Sports.

> *I sometimes work for my uncle who has a car-detailing business. I work there on Saturdays and mostly clean the outside of the cars and the hubcaps. This one Saturday, we were really busy, and this guy comes in at 12:00 and asks if we could do his car by 2:00 because he had this wedding or something. I thought No way. But my uncle says Okay, because I think he was a friend. So my uncle tells me to do the whole car, and I never usually do the insides. So I said Okay and started working first on the inside and then on the outside.*
>
> *When the guy came back at 2:00, the car was done, and he was real happy. He gave me a big tip. But what was really good was that I did the whole car in two hours. I was proud of that.*

Alex showed that he:

- Took on a project with a challenging deadline
- Planned what he had to do first
- Worked to meet the deadline and
- Completed the project and had a real sense of accomplishment.

Alex's interviewer wanted to know if he could meet a deadline. Alex thought about his work in his uncle's business in preparation for his interview and was able to give a good example. He showed that he took on a project even though at first he thought it couldn't get done on time and worked hard to complete it on time. He showed that he didn't complain about the tight time frame (even though at first he thought that he couldn't get the job done) and showed a positive attitude about doing the work. He also showed that he felt a real sense of accomplishment when he finished.

 TIP: Remember that when you give examples, be positive and show what you've accomplished.

***

Teamwork

***

Luis

Luis was asked at his interview, *Can you tell me about a time when a team member needed support? What was the situation? How did you know that this person needed support? What happened? What did you learn from this experience?*

Last year I worked part-time stacking shelves at the ABC Supermarket. I worked three hours a night, five days a week. There were four of us on the team. Every night we had to organize the products that were delivered in the back of the store and then organize how we were going to get them on the shelves.

One of the guys kept messing up—you know, putting the wrong items on the shelf. That was strange, because he was always pretty good at that. So I kind of wondered if something was wrong, and so I asked him. But he was pretty quiet at first but then said that his mom was ill and he had been taking her to the hospital for some appointments. I asked him how much longer his mom needed to go to the hospital, and he said two more weeks.

So I asked him if I could tell the other guys, and he said okay. Then we decided that for the next two weeks he could stock the water and soda and snack aisles. This was considered the easiest, because the products are pretty big and easy to get on the right shelf. We decided not to say anything to our supervisor because this change was only for two weeks and we were responsible for organizing how we wanted to work. I guess I learned that as a team we can take care of one of us and still meet our targets.

Teamwork means that you work willingly in a team and that you understand your own contribution to team success.

Luis showed that he is a team player and that he understands what it means to be in a team because he:

- Spoke positively about teamwork
- Showed an awareness of the business goal
- Identified a member in need of support and asked if he needed help
- Asked if he could share information with others and
- Took leadership action with the team to support team member.

Luis gave an example of working in a team. He used an example from last year and showed that he was comfortable being part of a team and that he understood different roles. He recognized that one team member needed some support, talked with him, and asked if he could share the information with the others. He also showed an awareness of achieving the team goal.

The interviewer chose this question to ask Luis because she saw on his résumé that he had worked in a team in the supermarket.

 Tip: Make sure you're prepared to answer questions that relate to all your experiences on your résumé.

***

***

Jessica
Jessica wanted an internship with a cybersecurity company.

Her interviewer also saw from her résumé that she had done an internship with the county police department, and she want to know Jessica's experience of teamwork.

She asked, *Can you tell me about a time when you were part of a team? What was the team, and what did you learn?*

Last semester I had an internship with the county police depart-ment. I was part of a group training in cybercrimes. We had to do a number of team activities, especially in looking at information and deciding what was relevant. In one exercise we had to determine if the information we had was factual, and so we had to look at where the information came from and how good the source was.

Each of us had to present our evaluation of the source to each other, and we had to listen to each other and decide the accuracy of the information.

We were better able to make the right determination as a team because there was more than one person giving his or her evalua-tion. We did really well in that exercise because we listened to one another and were open to different ideas.

Jessica showed that she:

- Spoke positively about the team
- Listened to others
- Used information gathered to make the right call and
- Learned that you get a better result as a team than as an individual.

Jessica used her previous internship as an example of teamwork. She showed that she listened to others and used what she learned to help make a decision. She realized that by working together and sharing information the team was able to make the right call.

 Tip: Don't be afraid to talk about your experience in another internship.

***

MORE ON COMMUNICATION: THE TELEPHONE INTERVIEW

Your interviewer will be assessing your communication skills from the moment she meets you face-to-face. However, sometimes you may have an interview on the phone. So you need to be prepared for that. Make sure you have notes in front of you that have key facts about yourself. Also have your elevator speech—not to read aloud, but to refer to if you're asked to describe yourself and what you want to do.

Interviewing by phone can be difficult. This is because you cannot see the person to whom you're talking. You can't read facial expressions, and you can't make eye contact. And you need to listen carefully so you understand the question. So you need to have your key points in front of you so you don't have long pauses or start saying things like "Well, umm . . ."

Remember, whether your interview is face-to-face or by phone, your interviewer will be assessing your ability to:

- Speak clearly
- Ask questions for information
- Listen
- Show enthusiasm and
- Make positive statements about yourself and others.

AWKWARD QUESTIONS

Every interview is different, and every interviewer has her own style. Remember, the reason for the interview is to get to know you better. And sometimes an interviewer may ask some questions to see how you might react.

Tips on Answering Difficult or Awkward Questions about Negative Feelings

1. Question: *Tell me about your least-favorite teacher or professor.*

> **TIP:** Don't take the bait! The interviewer is not inter-ested in who this person is but how you talk about him. Choose an example and briefly touch upon it and then quickly focus on what you learned from the experience. We all have had teachers or professors that we found difficult. But now is not the time to complain about them.

2. QUESTION: *Tell me about a problem you've had with a classmate or work colleague.*

> **TIP:** Again, don't fall for the bait. Don't start talking about a personality clash or any thing this individual may have done to annoy you. Instead, recognize that people have different ways of working and that this may have caused some issues. But show how you overcame those issues.

When an interviewer asks these questions, she wants to know if you too easily express negative feelings. Stay positive, and don't fall for the bait. Don't start expressing everything you don't like about a teacher or classmate or colleague.

Tips on Answering Difficult or Awkward Questions about Difficult Times

1. QUESTION: *Why aren't your grades better?*

> **TIP:** The interviewer wants to know how you handle disappointment. Be careful not to blame the school, col-lege, or teachers. Put a positive spin on your answer—like, "I learned a lot in many of my classes, and I always participated in class discussions. But I know that I could have worked harder."

2. QUESTION: *What course have you found most challenging and why?*

> **Tip:** The interviewer wants to know how well you respond to difficulty. Show that you don't quit when the going gets tough. And show that you're willing to put in the extra effort needed to succeed.

If your interviewer asks these questions, she wants to know how you handle difficult situations. What do you do to get through any disappointments? Are you willing to put in any effort you need to succeed?

Tips on Answering Difficult or Awkward Questions about Self-Awareness

1. QUESTION: *Why haven't you participated in more extracurricular activities?*

> **Tip:** The interviewer may be concerned that you don't have outside interests. Be sure your résumé shows the interests you have. You could say, for example, that although you did not join the track team you really like running and run at least five days a week. Or you may enjoy collecting sixties music and often go to flea markets to find the original vinyl records.

2. QUESTION: *What is your biggest weakness?*

> **Tip:** This is often a favorite question. It is best to own up and admit a weakness and not say, "Oh, I don't know" or "I don't have any." Choose a weakness, and show how you've overcome the problem. Be honest. Don't talk about a weakness that's made up. Take the time to give this question some thought.

Here, the interviewer wants to know how well you know yourself. Be honest. She'll know if you're making up some answers.

Don't be afraid of any difficult or awkward questions. She is not there to trip you up or trick you. The interviewer just wants to know how you handled any difficulties you may have faced.

WHEW—IT'S OVER!

You got through your interview and answered some difficult questions. But it is not over.

Your interviewer may ask if you have any questions. Remember to have at least two questions so that you show your interest in the internship.

When the interview is finished, she might say something like, "Thank you for coming in to see us. We will contact you in a few days."

Now is your time to thank your interviewer for seeing you and let her know that you're looking forward to hearing from her.

And don't forget . . . even though you thanked your interviewer, you'll want to write a short thank-you e-mail or note. You'll want to thank her again for her time and tell her that you're interested in the internship and that you look forward to hearing from her.

Now you can relax.

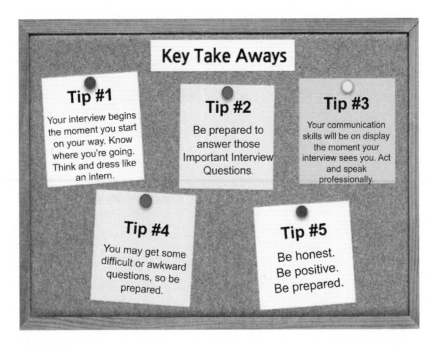

⑤

Get Off to a Good Start

Congratulations! You found an internship! Right now you're probably feeling pretty excited about the opportunity, and you're ready to get started. Everyone feels first-day jitters at the start of a new experience. This is an exciting time, and you want to get going.

It's natural to feel excitement and anticipation about this new situation. All interns have these types of feelings before they get into the actual activities of the internship. There are lots of questions: *What should I bring? What should I wear? Do you think I'll get lunch? What should I do? What should I say?*

You'll probably spend your first few days getting to know the work place and the people there and exploring what the business or organization is all about.

When you actually begin to work at your internship site, you may feel overwhelmed by the amount of new information coming at you. You may feel awkward, nervous, and totally dependent on your supervisor. And that's okay. That's what your supervisor is there for.

FIRST-DAY NERVES

If you expect the first-day jitters, you won't be surprised by feelings of excitement. If you're well prepared, things will go well.

***

Jessica
Jessica was really anxious her first day. Even though she had previously done an internship, this was a totally new setting.

The first day I arrived almost forty-five minutes early. I had to walk around and around the block and had so many coffees I was twice as jittery as I was just being early. Even though I had taken some courses that gave me some background for this internship, I really felt lost. Everyone seemed so smart and so busy, and what they were doing seemed so important. I was really mentally freaking out.

Jessica's experience is not unique. Everyone gets the first-day jitters. Jessica was smart to arrive early, even if she did have to walk around the neighborhood for a while. She might have been calmer just sitting down somewhere and reading something rather then drinking coffee and pacing around the neighborhood.

 Tip: Plan to be early so you can be right on time, but not too early so that you get more nervous waiting around.

***

Getting There

Make sure you know how to get to your internship site on time. You don't want to be late the first day. Even though you probably had an interview there, it might have been at a time of day when there wasn't much traffic or you traveled in a car and now you'll be taking public transportation or vice versa. Allow for mix-ups and traffic tie-ups. You don't want to come racing in at the last minute.

***

Michelle
Michelle's friend had driven her to her interview, but most of the time she was going to have to get herself there by public transportation, which was not that great in her town.

When I knew I had the internship, I started worrying about how I was going to get there on time every day. . . . There was a bus, but it was often late, and then coming home it was even later. I ran into my guidance counselor, and she suggested I talk with the supervisor right away about it rather than waiting until the last minute. When I called her, she was really nice. She said that it was okay with her if I varied my schedule from week to week if I took the work I was responsible for into consideration and let her know my plans.

She also pointed out that many of the events that we would be working on would be on weekends and evenings when I might get rides from friends. Also, she said the bus was not as bad as I had thought. The previous intern had used it and it worked out fine. Sometimes at the end of the day or evening the hotel's courtesy bus was free and would be able to drop me off at the end of my street.

Michelle approached what she thought would be a problem the best way—directly with her supervisor before she even began the internship. She was able to work out her transportation issues to everyone's satisfaction and had one less thing to worry about.

> **TIP:** It's best to work out transportation problems even before you accept the internship. The supervisor and sponsor can help a lot because they have probably dealt with this issue before.

***

Introductions, Handshakes, and Explaining Who You Are

In the business world, meeting new people involves a handshake. This is something you should have been practicing all along. People like a good firm handshake and a direct look into the eyes . . . but they don't like to feel that the other person is trying to wrestle them to the ground. And nobody is impressed by a limp handshake.

It is always acceptable to extend your hand first instead of waiting for others. Practice a few phrases like, "It's nice to meet you Ms. Smith. My name is Michelle Reddington. I'll be an intern in the events department for the next six months."

I HAVE A LOT OF QUESTIONS

What Should I wear?

The type of internship placement you have should determine your style of dress. However, businesses do not expect young people to have a large wardrobe of business or special attire. Just realize that your clothing should be comfortable and appropriate to the setting and that you should look well groomed. Comfortable clothing does not mean sloppy dress. And you'll be working, not going to a party.

How Can I Remember Everyone?

You'll probably forget half the people you meet the first few days. Don't worry too much about this. Some people have nameplates on their desks or doors to their offices or cubicles. Some wear nametags. If you really can't remember someone's name or if you haven't been introduced yet, you can always extend your hand and say something like "Hello, my name is Luis Belen. I'm an intern in the design department. I don't think we've met yet."

What Should I Bring?

Until you get your workspace set up, bring a notebook or legal pad and several decent pens with caps with you. You'll be taking a lot of notes. After you're settled, you'll have these things in your desk or workstation. Don't expect to use your cell phone or tablet to type in the information you'll receive the first few days. It may be easy for you, but it also may be perceived as rude for you to be hunched over a device, typing, while someone is talking with you.

You should also bring a copy of your résumé with you. You can never tell when someone may ask for it. And keep a clean copy in a folder in your desk . . . once you get a desk. If you have a tote bag or messenger bag, that can be handy until you get an official place to keep your things.

What if I Get Hungry?

Depending on the scheduled hours of your internship, bring a snack and small drink (water or juice) and a piece of fruit. This will be helpful until you figure out the break and lunch situation. Some businesses have cafeterias, and in others people go out to buy their lunches. You don't have to feel that you need to spend money on eating out just because others do so. It is perfectly acceptable to eat in the break or lunch room. Be careful about eating at your desk. Not only is it messy and unprofessional, the business may not allow it. Also, don't bring large, messy, noisy bags of snacks like tortilla chips or Cheetos.

Um, Where Do I Sit?

Your supervisor will be expecting you on your first day and has probably already arranged where you'll sit and keep your belongings. If not, you'll need to ask.

About Desks

You may find that you'll be sharing a desk with someone else who is using that space when you aren't there. If this is the case, make sure that you leave the workspace in neat condition when you finish work for the day. As an additional note, just as your desk is for *you*, your coworkers' desks are theirs. *Never* open drawers or take anything from someone else's desk or answer their phones without permission.

MEETING WITH YOUR SUPERVISOR

Usually you'll have a basic getting-to-know-each-other meeting with your supervisor or mentor on the first day.

***

Luis

Luis was very concerned about getting off to a good start both with his supervisor and coworkers.

On the first day I was there, I was able to meet with my supervisor and get a lot of information and get some questions answered. I also talked with him about how I should work with everyone else in the office and if they thought I was an employee or what. He explained that they knew I was there as an intern and that all of them had been the "new guy" at one time or another and that I should feel free to ask anyone any questions I had . . . that I didn't have to wait to ask him.

That made me feel pretty good since I knew I'd have a lot of questions in the coming days.

You might be concerned about how other people in the workplace will treat you, but you don't have to be. Other people know that you're an intern, and most of them will be very helpful. People are usually proud of their work and enjoy teaching someone new how things are done.

TIP: If you're interested in what other people are doing and ask them a lot of questions about their work, most coworkers will be happy to help you out.

***

I Have Some More Questions

On the first day, you'll be covering a lot of topics. Some important items are on the list in EXTRA INFO 5A: Make Sure You Know . . . at the end of this chapter. Review the list to make sure you've covered all of the items. In addition to the items on the checklist, interns also need to know:

- The supervisor's daily schedule. You need to ask who keeps the supervisor's daily calendar and how you should schedule time to meet. Some places are much more informal than others, and you need to know this up front.
- Whether or not you can schedule a standing weekly meeting. Things will get busy very quickly and the time you have during the initial days with your supervisor will become shorter and shorter. A standing meeting assures that you'll be able to count on a set period of time to discuss projects, progress and clarification on issues if needed.

- How you should address your supervisor. You don't want to call your supervisor Carol if everyone else addresses her as Mrs. Smith. You may have already figured this out just by listening to how people address her as you were introduced around the office. But try to figure this out as soon as possible.
- How your supervisor prefers you communicate with him—e-mail? Text? In person? Regular meetings? If the door is open, is it alright for you to assume your supervisor is free?
- Exactly what your schedule is. Review the schedule you discussed at your interview, and make sure the times discussed are still workable.
- Does the rest of the office staff know what your role is? If everyone knows who you are, you don't have to keep explaining it. Also, if the rest of the staff knows who you are and who your supervisor is, they may be less likely to view you as a possible assistant. You can learn a lot from all of the people who work in a business or organization. Clarify if it is okay to ask various people to talk with your from time to time about their particular jobs.
- Where everyone eats lunch. Perhaps in a tour of the site you've seen a lunchroom or cafeteria or just a break room and you don't need to ask this question. But do clarify this. Ask if there is a refrigerator if you bring your lunch and learn the routine for using the lunch or break room (such as taking turns cleaning out the fridge, putting names on things, etc.).
- About where supplies are. Some organizations and businesses have one person who is the gatekeeper of all supplies. Others are less formal, and people just help themselves to what they need. It is important to determine what the situation is before you need something. If there is one person in charge of supplies, it is a pretty good idea to make that person your new best friend.

THE FIRST FEW DAYS

Telephones

The phones on the desks are office phones. They are for the business, not for anyone's personal use. Your own cell phone, of course, should be locked in your desk for the duration of your work time. This means you won't be on the phone except for business during your internship hours.

One of the first things you'll need to familiarize yourself with will be the telephone system. This is probably something that an office manager or your supervisor or an assistant will be able to show you. Make sure you take accurate notes, because for businesses and organizations the telephones are still a main line to business.

As an intern you'll frequently need to use the telephone for business, which is quite different than using the telephone for social reasons.

There are standard business telephone practices that you should review before you begin to answer the phones for other people and for your own work there.

Answering the Telephone

Just saying "Hello" or "Hi" is not appropriate. You should ask how the telephone in your internship is officially answered, write it down, and keep it with you in your desk. Listen to how others answer the phone, and try to answer yours in the same manner.

Taking Accurate Messages

Nothing is more exasperating than an incomplete or confusing message. It is easy to get things wrong when the phones are ringing, people are talking, printers are printing, and you can barely hear on the phone.

Make sure you write down all information accurately. Don't be afraid to ask someone to repeat information.

Computer Etiquette

The company's computers are for the company's work . . . not your personal e-mail, Facebook, Tweets, or personal searches. Period.

Other Office Machines and Technology

Before you use something, make sure you know how. Don't be afraid to ask someone how the copy machine works or how the printer works. Even if you've used these before, each is different, and there is nothing

more embarrassing than jamming up the copier—even though everyone does it at some time or another.

NOW WHAT DO I DO?

***

Jessica

After Jessica's nerve-wracking beginning, the rest of her first day
wasn't so bad. Luckily, her supervisor had arranged a place for her, and
she was able to settle down quickly into her own space.

> *Thanks to my supervisor I could sit down and catch my breath. He
> gave me some things to read right away so I at least had something
> to do to take my mind off being nervous.*
>
> *From where I was sitting I could also see that some of the other
> people looked close to my age and they all seemed to be friendly with
> each other. That made me feel a little better.*

Jessica's supervisor also had some things for her to read on her first
day. She could settle down and get involved reading and didn't have to
sit and wait for someone to tell her what to do next. It's a good idea to
bring some reading material with you at the beginning of your internship so you don't have to sit awkwardly trying to look busy.

 TIP: Remember, now you're an active learner. Don't just sit
around and wait for someone to tell you what to do.

***

Your supervisor may already have some projects to get started on, or
you both may have decided before the internship began that you would
work on specific tasks, and that's good.

Check out chapter 6 of this book to see five things you can work on
at *any* internship.

Talk to your supervisor about attending meetings. Most businesses and organizations do a lot of their business through meetings . . . meetings to share information, meetings for trainings and professional development, meetings for talking about new ideas and new practices, and meetings to resolve difficulties or problems. You can learn a great deal at meetings, especially if you come prepared.

Read the agenda, and ask your supervisor about items you don't understand. Research the topic if you can, either online or through the company files. Learn about who is involved, what departments are affected, and why.

Discuss the upcoming meeting with your supervisor to see if there is a particular goal they might have in mind. Taking accurate notes and reporting back would be a good use of your time at the meeting. Or just listening and observing will add to your company knowledge.

You can learn a lot just by observing people, their actions, inactions, demeanor, and participation in meetings.

Ask Questions

Show your enthusiasm for learning by asking a lot of questions. Too many interns are afraid of being pests or of bothering people with too many questions. People like to talk about themselves and their work.

Don't forget, you're primarily there to learn, and if you don't ask questions, people will assume you don't have any. If you're eager to learn, don't feel shy about requesting explanations. Be inquisitive from day one. Ask people if you can help them with a project, if you still don't have a lot to do. Ask people for help with something you're working on rather than waiting around for your supervisor to help. Ask people how they started working here.

***

Alex
At first Alex felt that he could only ask questions of his supervisor, but one day at the beginning of his internship he was really getting busy and found himself working with a customer and needed some parts to complete the job he was doing.

Right in the middle of helping this kid fix his wheels on his board, I realized I needed some parts, and since he was anxious to get back outside with his friends, I didn't want to wait until my supervisor came back from lunch to ask him. . . . I was really nervous, but I had to ask one of the salesmen who didn't seem busy.

He was really great. . . . He took me in the back and showed me a storage room where they had all sorts of things. After I finished help-ing the kids, I went back to check out everything that was in there in case I needed to find things later.

That salesman later told me he had started as a stock clerk and he knew where everything was in the store. . . . So I guess I picked the right person to ask this time.

Alex was able to ask for help from a coworker and learned a lot about where things were kept in the bargain.

> **TIP:** Your supervisor is not the only person who can help you and answer your questions. If others are not in the middle of something, they will probably be more than willing to help you out and explain things. They were new once too.

***

If you still aren't really comfortable asking questions, perhaps clarifying with your supervisor when he prefers to be asked questions would help. Perhaps they would like you to ask things all at once rather then as they come up, or perhaps they prefer answering things on the fly. Ask. You'll never know if you don't ask.

THINGS ARE GETTING BUSY FAST

After the first few days that may seem slow to you, you may find that things around your workplace are really heating up. Projects and reports are due. Clients are coming in and calling. And you're pretty much past the orientation phase and into the actual business of learning the business. Projects may have advanced on the days you're not scheduled to be there, so you'll need to check on any updates and make sure you're on the same page as everyone else involved.

It won't take long before you begin to feel that coming to your internship is just a natural part of your schedule, and soon the people there will treat you like you've been there forever.

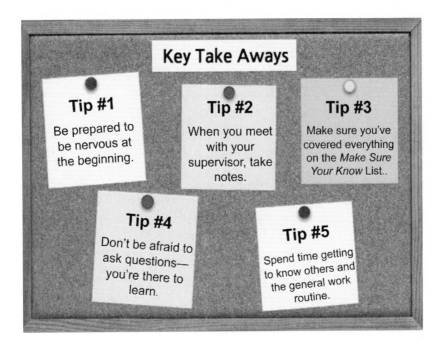

Key Take Aways

Tip #1
Be prepared to be nervous at the beginning.

Tip #2
When you meet with your supervisor, take notes.

Tip #3
Make sure you've covered everything on the *Make Sure Your Know* List..

Tip #4
Don't be afraid to ask questions—you're there to learn.

Tip #5
Spend time getting to know others and the general work routine.

EXTRA INFO 5A: Make Sure You Know

Location of your

- ☐ Desk, chair and place to keep
  papers, files and supplies (and key(s)
  if needed)

Who is who

- ☐ Overall tour of site
- ☐ Introductions to key staff

Workplace Information

- ☐ Location of rest rooms (and key if
  needed)
- ☐ Lunch/break facility
- ☐ Parking
- ☐ Where to store personal belongings

Workplace Details:

- ☐ Telephone number and address of
  site
- ☐ Confirmation of work schedule
  hours
- ☐ Break times
- ☐ Lunch break
- ☐ Location of time clock or sign in
- ☐ Working with other departments,
  branches, and co-workers.
- ☐ Who to call when absent or late

Job Specific

- ☐ How to use the phones
- ☐ How to use the office equipment
- ☐ Location of important files
- ☐ Location of supplies (paper, pens,
  notepads, etc.)

Safety Procedures

- ☐ What to do in an emergency
- ☐ Location of stairs
- ☐ Location of fire exits
- ☐ Location of fire extinguishers
- ☐ Evacuation routes
- ☐ Fire alarms and fire alarm testing

Standards:

- ☐ Dress code (clothing, hair, footwear,
  etc.)
- ☐ Work performance (productivity,
  work habits)
- ☐ Company culture (team work,
  customer service, values)
- ☐ Security and confidentiality issues

Company Information:

- ☐ Copy of personnel handbook
- ☐ Staff telephone directory
- ☐ Key people in the company
- ☐ Who your customers or clients will
  be

6

Get the Most Out of Your Internship

Now that you've started your internship, you'll want to know how to get the most from it. There are some things that you can do to make sure you get value out of the time and effort you're putting into your internship.

6 THINGS TO GET THE MOST OUT OF YOUR INTERNSHIP

First, get and use a mentor. Second, find ways to turn "grunt work" into real work. Third, independently work on projects that will add value to your internship. Fourth, identify and build those skills that every employer and college wants. Fifth, listen and learn from other interns. And sixth and finally, keep a journal or write a blog.

WHAT CAN A MENTOR DO FOR YOU?

If you're part of an internship program in your school or college, you probably will be assigned a mentor at your internship site. If you've found your internship independently, you'll want to ask someone at your internship site to become your mentor.

A mentor acts as your counselor, guide, tutor, or coach as you continue through your internship. Your mentor may be your supervisor or may be someone in your organization who is interested in your internship.

A mentor allows and encourages you to participate in activities that may not be open to entry-level employees, such as staff meetings or client consultations. This gives you a broad view of your organization. This also gives you the opportunity to observe managers and leaders in action and helps you to identify some of the leadership skills that are key to success.

A mentoring relationship will help you to reflect on your experience in a supportive environment and gives you the opportunity to ask questions. Often the mentor can pass on a wealth of experience and knowledge.

**

Jessica
When Jessica started her internship, she asked if she would have a mentor. She was told that the human-resources manager would be her mentor.

> *I was really happy that I asked about a mentor on my first day. I was told that it would be the HR person who interviewed me. When we met up, she said that while she was not in my department I could talk with her if I had any questions or problems. And she told me she would show me around the company and tell me about all the projects that were happening.*
>
> *She also said she would make sure that I got included in department meetings as well as any training sessions that were held. I had been a little nervous that I would be on my own, but after that conversation I felt so much better.*

A mentor is key if you want to learn the most from your internship experience. He can be the person who suggests projects, helps you set goals, and helps you reflect on what you're learning. He can also run interference if you find that the activities you're spending your time on are not meeting your expectations.

**

SPEAKING OF "GRUNT WORK"

One thing you need to keep in mind: *every* job has grunt work. You're not being singled out.

What is Grunt Work?

Grunt work is work that's sometimes viewed as routine, seemingly insignificant, monotonous, and not very creative or inspiring. It can also be called

- Donkey work
- Menial work
- Scut work and
- Being a gofer.

Please don't get the idea that the tasks listed as examples of grunt work are demeaning or that you should never do them. The problem with grunt work comes when it takes up a great deal of time during your internship and you end up doing these tasks over and over to the exclusion of doing other more meaningful work.

Examples of Grunt Work

Grunt work usually entails things like:

- Answering phones
- Filing documents
- Organizing files
- Making and collating copies and presentations
- Organizing supply closets
- Making coffee or cleaning up after meetings
- Going out to get coffee/lunch/snacks/dry cleaning/newspapers
- Loading equipment
- Setting up equipment
- Cleaning up a work site and
- Running errands.

What Can I Learn from Grunt Work?

There is a bigger picture—and you are now a part of it.

You may think there is nothing to learn from doing mundane, everyday tasks, but if you look beyond the task itself and think about how it fits into the company or organization's purpose, then you'll see the larger picture and where the work fits in. Take a little time to think about how what you're being asked to do supports the larger organization and what you can learn from doing the task. For example:

- Proofreading and collating PowerPoints could provide you with some insight into important work going on.
- Working the phones or responding to inquiry e-mails can help you develop a sense about the public's view of where you're interning and what is happening there.
- Inventorying and stocking supplies can help you see the budgetary side of this business.
- Checking documents and filing can give you insight into a wider understanding of the company's activities and client needs.
- Even getting the coffee orders delivered correctly can provide networking opportunities. As you drop off each order, you'll have a chance to meet people, especially senior people. Introduce yourself, ask a question, or just make a good impression.

What to do When There is too Much Grunt Work

In general, people at your site will be very supportive and helpful. They're proud of the work they do and are happy to help someone younger explore careers and learn new skills.

Occasionally, others view a new intern's arrival as an opportunity to move some of their work onto the intern's desk.

Sometimes you just have to do it. But not all the time. If your mentor or supervisor has assigned the grunt work tasks, that's one thing. If other people in the workplace are "assigning" you tasks, that isn't so fine.

In the spirit of being a team player, it might be good to just do the grunt work for a short period. But if it becomes routine and consumes most of your time, you need to say no professionally.

How to Say No Professionally

There are ways to handle situations like this so that others don't take advantage of you. What you don't say is "I'm not your intern. You don't get to give me assignments."

What you *could* say is something like, "I'd like to help you; however, right now I'm [doing something for my mentor or finishing this project/assignment or just about to start on this review that is due soon . . .]. If I have time when I finish, I'll let you know, and maybe I can help you then."

This assumes you've got some work on your desk and aren't just sitting and staring at nothing.

Look at the projects mentioned later in this chapter, the ones that can be done at any internship. Work on those if you don't have another assignment at the moment.

And then make an appointment to talk to your mentor or supervisor about refocusing the time you're spending there.

How to Move from too Much Grunt Work to Real Work

If it has been a week or so and you're still spending your time making copies, collating documents, and organizing files, it is time to talk with your mentor, supervisor, or school about finding more challenging activities.

Hopefully you sat down with your mentor at the beginning of your internship and set several site-specific goals and listed activities that you would do to learn more about this career area and try out the work involved. If so, it is time to bring out those goals and see what current work and projects you can get involved with to help you achieve them.

If this was not done before you began your internship, then now is the time to do it. Your mentor or supervisor is the person to help you set goals and get involved in projects and activities.

But you also have to contribute ideas. If you've noticed people working on a specific project that interests you, ask if you might become involved in the team working on that. If there are computer programs used in your workplace, make it a goal to learn one or two of them while you're there. Ask to work on key projects and to attend meetings, just so you know what is going on. You have to take some of the initiative at this point. No one can read your mind.

While you're beginning to assume more responsibility and do more meaningful work, you may still have to do an occasional bit of grunt work. Some of it may even be related to projects you're working on. It's all part of the learning experience.

FIVE PROJECTS TO MAKE THE MOST OF DOWNTIME

Yes, there will be downtime. And you don't want to be sitting around doing nothing. This is the time you can take responsibility and work on some of your own projects.

When you have some downtime, talk with your mentor about your thoughts and ask for his thoughts and suggestions, since he's the person actually working there. Your mentor may already have some projects planned for you. Tell him there are some projects you would like to work on that will help you better understand the company or organization.

Start with the following five projects, and see how you get on:

#1: What is Everyone Reading Here? (Literature in the Field)

Every career area has its own informational sources, either print or electronic.

First, ask you mentor, supervisor, or colleagues what magazines or journals there are specific to the industry or field. Check to see if there are magazines or journals available for you to look at. Second, you probably have access to a computer at work, at school, or at home. Use the Internet to look for articles, news stories, journals, and magazines relating you to your organization or your internship field.

Keep a record of what you've read. You can refer to this information if you do a presentation about your internship at school. You can also refer to it if you're writing a blog for others to read.

#2: How did These People End Up Here? (Career Path)

The varied answers to that question will probably surprise you. Interview your mentor and supervisor, and take the time to ask your colleagues about their careers. Some questions you can ask:

- What is your specific job?
- How did you come to be doing this job?

- What preparation did you have to have?
- How did you learn your specific job here?
- What degrees and certifications are needed?
- Did you enter this career the traditional way or some other?

To learn more about a person's job, you may want to ask your mentor if you can job shadow an individual employee. You can take notes on your observation, as this will help you to better understand the organization's structure.

***

Luis
Luis wanted to know more about his CEO at City Net Design.

I really wanted to know how the CEO got his job. I was surprised to learn that he didn't major in graphics or Web design in college. His major was marketing, but he had a real interest in computers and design. He worked in marketing for a while but then joined a graphics-design start-up and did a variety of things.

He said his major challenge was not in the technical side of the business but in managing people. Because he focused on building the business and getting the right people, his company became very successful and was bought by City Net Design in New York. He has stayed on as CEO and is now working in a larger company than he started.

Before I interviewed him, I never even knew how important managing people is to the success of a business.

Luis learned that his CEO's interest in computers and design and experience in marketing helped him get his job in a graphics-design start-up. He also learned that his CEO willingly took on a variety of activities, which helped him learn about the graphics-design business. He discovered that even in a technical field managing people was important to success.

***

#3: Who is Who, and Who is in Charge Here?
(Organizational Structure)

In any place of work, there is an organizational structure—from a two-person office, to a family business, a start-up company, an educational establishment, a charity, a hospital, or a multinational corporation.

It is important to know where you and your internship fit. You'll find out more by researching the organization and interviewing the leaders.

First, use the Internet to find information. Most organizations, no matter the field, have a website. As you search the website, you'll find information about the history, the founder, the employees, the values, and the purpose of the organization.

Second, interview the leaders in the organization. These may be members of the senior management team, your department head, human-resources professionals, or an administrator.

Some questions you can ask:

- When did this company or organization begin?
- How was it founded?
- What is the purpose (why does it exist)?
- What is its size, and how has it grown?
- What value does it bring to the community?
- Does this organization have competitors? If so, who are they?
- What are the challenges facing this organization and/or industry today and in the future?

Keep notes on your interview and research. They will help you to describe your internship in more detail for a school or college project or in future job and college interviews.

#4: What do These Weird Words Mean? (Vocabulary)

So many career areas have unique vocabulary or terminology. In order to function well in a given field you need to learn this "language."

Create a list of unfamiliar words and phrases. These may be technical words or acronyms (made up words that refers to a process, policy, or way of doing things).

Ask your colleagues to help you define these terms, and use the Internet to find out more about their meaning.

#5: What's Happening in Social Media?

Almost every organization today has a presence online. Organizations want to know what their customers are thinking, or they want to be sure they know the latest trends. Or they want their message to get out to as many people as possible.

As a young person you're likely more comfortable with social media than some other more senior people at your internship. Some things you can do to know more about what's happening in your organization's field and to add value are:

- List social media that people are using today.
- Check with your supervisor as to what social media your organization is currently using. You might suggest some others that could be of value.
- Look at what people are saying about your organization on Twitter, Facebook, and other channels. Write a short summary of your findings.
- If your organization monitors social media, ask if you can see their Web analytics.
- Develop a plan for the best use of social media for your organization.

Even if your organization is comfortable with their current position regarding social media, you can use your research to talk about this project in a presentation, future job, and college interviews.

***

Alex
Alex was surprised when his manager asked him to look at the store's website and social media and suggest ways to attract more young people.

My manager asked me one day if I used social media. Seriously! So he asked me to think of some ways that they could get younger people to come into the store. So I looked at their Facebook page and told them some things to change, especially in some of the "old fashioned" words they use to describe sports and equipment. I also told them to make the pictures on their website more realistic so kids would like them.

Funny thing is they took my advice and made some changes. I was surprised but felt really good about it.

Like Alex, you may be asked to do something you think is not part of your internship. Do it. You're being asked because your supervisor or manager thinks you can help. And the experience may open up some new doors for your talents.

***

 TIP: Choose the projects that interest you. You don't need to do all five, but do an in-depth job on the ones you choose.

IT'S NOT JUST THE PROJECTS

Your internship is a great way for you to build the skills needed for your future success. Some people call these skills *life skills*. Others call them *soft skills*. Another refers to them as *survival skills*. These are the skills that every employer and college wants you to have. Whatever you call them, they're essential for your future.

Communication, Teamwork, and Work Ethic (Again)!

Many organizations and colleges think that these three skills and attitudes are the most important ones for their employees or students to have mastered. You may have been asked about these skills at your interview. There the interviewer was simply interested in your awareness of teams and meeting deadlines. And the interviewer would be listening to how you communicated your ideas.

But after your internship you'll have specific examples of how you worked in a team, showed a can-do attitude, set goals, and met deadlines. You'll also have more self-confidence when you talk about your experience, as you now can show specific examples.

How to Strengthen These Three Critical Skills

Now that you know what skills are important, you have a great opportunity to show them in action.

Communication

Every organization, college, and university wants to know that their employees or students can communicate clearly and to the point. So when you think about your communication skills, be sure you try to do the following:

- Speak clearly, and don't mumble.
- Ask questions to get more information.
- Listen to what others have to say.
- Be enthusiastic about your ideas.
- Tell others what is happening.
- Talk about others in a positive way.

Teamwork

You may wonder why this is so important. Whether you're in a job or at university you'll be working in a team. At work your team may be your work colleagues with whom you work to complete a task. At university your team may be your classmates working on a class project. Either way you'll be expected to understand how a team works, what your role is, and the role of other team members and to be able to handle any conflict that might arise. So what does teamwork look like today?

Having good team-working skills means that you're able to work willingly in a group and with others and that you understand your own contribution to the team's success.

So when you look at how you work in a team be sure you try to do the following:

- Give information to others in the team. Don't keep things secret from the others. Team success means that all team members share information so that the team can find the best solution to a problem.
- Treat other team members the way they want to be treated. If someone is shy, for example, try not to keep asking her to speak up in the team all the time, but instead ask her to talk about subjects that she knows about or is interested in.
- Be willing to help other team members.
- Be aware of how your own actions impact others on the team.

Remember, teams are made up of individuals. And individuals are not all alike.

Work Ethic

This is important because an employer or college wants to be sure that you're willing to do what it takes to get the job done.

Having a good work ethic means that you have a can-do outlook and that you want to succeed. So when you think about how you demonstrated your work ethic, think about the projects you completed and how you met a deadline. Can you show that you set goals for yourself and set priorities?

Be sure to ask yourself whether you:

- Keep time commitments. Getting to work or class on time and meeting deadlines are important here. Or are you always late?
- Manage your own time. Do you set goals for yourself? Do you prioritize all the things you had to do? Are you able to focus on the most important things?
- Try to do every activity or task "right the first time."
- "Own" your own work. If you make a mistake, do you admit it? Are you able to correct the mistake and move on?
- Ask questions if you're not clear about what needs to be done.

Tip: Keep some notes about how you showed these skills in you projects and work tasks. Keeping a record of how you continued to build and strengthen these skills will help you talk about them at job and college interviews.

FRIENDS CAN MAKE THE DIFFERENCE

Most schools and colleges that have an internship program or provide internships for their students also have a way for the students to share their experiences. This may be in a weekly class or seminar or in a less-formal group meeting where you meet with other interns. Whatever way it is done, be sure you are part of it.

***

Michelle
Michelle's school held seminars every other week for all the students who were doing an internship.

I really looked forward to the seminars. Sometimes I was so excited to share with the other students what I had been doing and what new things I was learning. That was great. And sometimes, especially if I messed up on something, I got some great advice from them and lots of support. It was also a good way for me to try out some new ideas and get some feedback.

Michelle was open about sharing her internship experience with others. She also was able to hear the suggestions from others. She felt supported in her internship.

***
***

Luis
Luis's college required that he attend a weekly class. It was a formal class where students gave presentations about various aspects of their internships.

At first, I really hated this class. I was so busy and would much rather have been at my internship. But it sometimes was helpful to hear what the others were doing. And sometimes I got some new ideas. And I gave a great presentation about my internship so that everyone wanted to work there. The one thing it did show me was how really good my internship was because I had a lot of freedom to work on projects even if I messed up.

Although Luis thought he would not get much from his class, he got to see how great his internship was by listening to others.

***

***

Alex

Alex's school had an informal arrangement about meetings.

There were like only six kids doing internships when I did one. We got together with the guidance counselor maybe every other week or so. I wasn't sure why we were meeting. But after a while when I listened to what the other interns were doing, I thought, "Wow— they're having the same problems I have." I guess this helped me to stay on with my internship since I really didn't like it that much. So maybe getting together is good to do.

Alex was able to see that other interns were facing some of the same issues that bothered him, and he saw that he was not alone in his feelings.

***

***

Jessica

Jessica was comfortable attending her college's internship seminars because she had already completed one internship. She used the time to get advice from other interns and to try out some new ideas.

My first internship didn't really have scheduled meetings, and I kind of like being able to talk with other interns about problems and to describe what I've been doing. It helps me see how much I'm learning. I got some good feedback from the others, and I felt good because I could help some of them, too.

Think about the time you've spent with your friends and classmates as part of your internship. What did you learn from them? How did they help you out? How were you able to help them out? What do you think they learned from you?

***

> Tip: Listening to other interns talk about their experiences lets you see that many interns share the same feelings you have. These conversations help you to see and understand the bigger picture of your internship.

KEEP A JOURNAL; WRITE A BLOG

Thinking about your internship as you go along from when you started to the time you finish will help you to refer to your experience in the future.

One of the best ways for you to know what you've accomplished in your internship is by keeping a journal or writing a blog about your experience. A journal is most often a private record that you may or may not wish to share.

On the other hand, you may want to write a blog about your experience for others to read.

Whatever way you choose to record your experience, the writing will help you to reflect on what is happening and will help you to organize your thoughts.

When your internship is finished, looking back over your journal or blogs will help you to pull together what you learned and include it on your résumé. Reading your writing, even months after your internship is over, will help you identify what you learned in the projects you completed, the teams you've worked in, the new ideas you considered. Reminding yourself of what you've learned will give you specific examples of what you've achieved and can be used as you go forward for job and college interviews.

What's in a Journal?

As you start your journal you can write about:

- How it feels to be in a new place
- What your workplace looks like and how you feel about it
- Who your colleagues are and the jobs they do
- The first tasks or projects you're doing
- What part of your work you find most interesting or what area of the organization interests you the most or
- Something new that you tried and what happened.

As you continue your journal—and remember, a journal is *private*—you may want to write about:

- A conflict or disappointed you've had or may be having
- A problem you may be experiencing
- What it feels like to be part of a team
- An outside problem (with family, friends, or schools) that may be causing you concern
- Something that happened at the internship that made you emotional
- What your internship has taught you about yourself
- What you accomplished and took the most pride in doing
- What skills you gained or
- Something new that you learned.

A journal is usually kept daily (or on the days that you're at your internship). You may write in it without worrying about grammar, spelling, or organization. And then read it through once and make any changes that will clarify your entry. Rereading your journal in the future will help you to remember all that you did and learned in your internship.

What about a Blog?

Blogs are *not* private. Remember, if you post a blog, it can be read by *anyone*, even if you think you're restricting it to your friends. Future employers and college-admissions counselors would not want to know that you may have complained about your internship or written negatively about your colleagues. So be careful.

Some students prefer to write a blog rather than a journal. But blogs take more time to get the writing right. You need to watch spelling, grammar, content, and tone. Remember, it is not private.

A blog can help you tell the story of your internship and can be of interest to others who may want to do an internship in the future. Or you can consolidate all of your blogs to show your full experience and learning at your internship. Your school may use your blog to grant you credit for your internship.

In your blog you could:

- Describe your first days at your internship. You might talk about what you expected and how the internship might be different.
- Describe the projects you're working on and how they're part of what other people are doing.
- Highlight what you're learning or have learned.
- Talk about your accomplishments and what gave you the most pride.
- Summarize the skills you've developed.
- Talk about your future plans and how you hope to achieve them.

Remember (we know, we can't say this enough) a blog is out there on the Internet, and anyone can find it and read it. You want to present a positive view of yourself and show potential readers what you've learned and how you want to use your knowledge in the future.

Whether you choose to write a journal or a blog, it is the writing down of your thoughts that will help you reflect on and integrate your experience.

Your internship will probably never be exactly what you planned—it will usually be better. Make the most of what there is to learn and do . . . Ask a lot of questions, keep notes and copies of your work, and enjoy it.

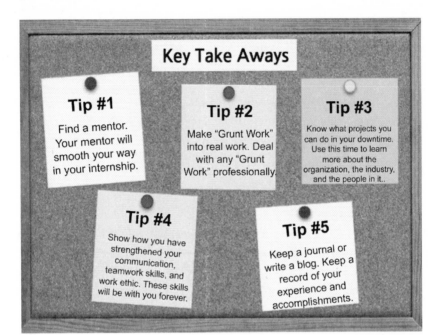

7

When Things Just Aren't Working Out

Doing an internship is not easy. You have to go to an unfamiliar place. You have to meet and work with new people. You have to add value to the business or organization and learn new skills. This can seem pretty overwhelming all at once. After the first few weeks you might even be thinking that you've made a mistake and that this might not be the right thing for you.

Don't worry! You're not alone! Probably every intern has had doubts and concerns more than once during his internship!

Every internship experience is different. It all depends on your personality, skills, interests, and learning style. All interns pass through normal cycles, moving from being a student who doesn't know all that much about the world of work, to someone who is gaining workplace skills and actively participating in the sponsor's organization.

It helps to be aware of the natural cycle of things—to understand the feelings and problems that can crop up—and to learn how to deal with things in a constructive way. You want the internship experience to be as successful as possible.

All positions have challenges, whether it's an internship now or a job later. Learning how to deal with challenges now will help you build your experience and skills for later!

WHEN THE NOVELTY WEARS OFF

It's new and exciting to arrange and prepare for an internship. Once you were accepted at an internship site, you probably had a lot of expectations.

When you actually began to work at your internship site you might have first felt overwhelmed by the amount of new information you had to remember. But the situation was still so new and exciting that you probably weren't too concerned.

You may have thought, "What could be a problem in this situation?" And usually there aren't that many. Except often people forget that most new things are usually pretty exciting, and then, one day, that novelty will wear off. That's when it is time to dig in and look for the deeper, less superficial things that made the situation exciting in the first place.

If you look closely at your initial internship expectations and compare them with the reality of what you're experiencing now, you can begin to see how this could lead to problems. Sometimes there is a disconnect between the excitement of starting out and the routine you're experiencing now.

When the cloud of reality drifts over and you begin to think, *"Uh, this internship isn't exactly what I thought it would be . . ."* it's time to sit down and breathe deeply, chill, and think hard about what's really bothering you.

AND THE GRIPING BEGINS

Have you started grumbling to friends that the internship is not what you expected? Are you beginning to question why things aren't so great? Are you griping that your supervisor doesn't like you or you're feeling like your head is going to explode because you have so many things to do?

Are you beginning to think that what you're feeling is wrong and that "good" interns don't think like this? If so, don't worry. It's normal.

You're beginning to see the difference between what you expected at the start of your internship and what the reality has turned out to be. And it's never the same.

You might not even be able to put a name to what you're feeling— frustration, anger, sadness, and disappointment may be all wrapped up in one big ball of confusion.

TIME TO FIGURE OUT WHAT'S GOING ON

Three main areas can sometimes cause problems during an internship:

- Supervisors and mentors
- Work assignments
- Juggling responsibilities.

Problems with Supervisors and Mentors

Usually problems with supervisors or mentors involve

- Too much or too little time together
- Not enough or confusing directions or
- Criticism and feedback.

Sometimes interns have a tendency to assume that supervisors know everything an intern is doing and how he feels. But that isn't fair to the supervisors. They're not mind readers and need to be told how you're doing and how you feel about things, because they may be too busy or may just forget to ask on a regular basis.

Working Out Time Problems

Sometimes it's easy for supervisors to forget that you're new to the workplace, and if they don't hear from you, they assume everything is fine. It's really important to reach out for help or to ask for time to talk when you need it. Don't let things go. You can set up weekly meetings with your supervisor so you can check in and make sure you're completing tasks correctly

Ask how they want you to keep in touch . . . daily e-mail? Once a week? Open-door policy? As things come up? Just make sure you're clear on what has been decided and comfortable with the decision and frequency.

Working Out Direction Problems

Sometimes supervisors assume that once you've done something once, you've got it. Or perhaps they give confusing directions and leave you unsure about things like due dates or methods for doing the work. If directions aren't clear, ask for more information if you aren't sure how to do something. If you prefer directions in writing, you'll need to ask for that.

Working Out Criticism and Feedback Problems

Some interns think corrections and suggestions for changes are a personal criticism. In the world outside of school, supervisors often suggest changes and constructively criticize work. The key words here are *constructive criticism.* This leaves an opening for discussion, revision, and fine-tuning of work and for personal growth.

Don't assume your supervisor is not happy with all of your work when he makes suggestions about redoing or correcting one part of an assignment. He's looking at specific tasks, not everything you're doing.

Ask for feedback as you go along. If you feel that will help you in what you do, you can just ask for more frequent feedback and suggestions for ways you can improve your work. Perhaps your supervisor didn't want to overload you or appear to be constantly hovering over you as you worked on something.

***

Luis

Luis seemed to fit right in with the company's culture after the first week of getting to know everyone.

At first, my supervisor took me all around and introduced me to everyone and told them about my experience and why I was there. He explained that I would be working on projects on two different teams, and it made me feel really included when he did that. And then, after the first week, he seemed to disappear. I missed a meeting waiting to meet with him.

Finally when we did sit down to talk and I told him what had happened, he said that he had assumed I was settled in and didn't need him to be ushering me around anymore. I told him that I would appreciate being able to check in with him regularly, so we scheduled a weekly appointment, and he told me to e-mail him if I had urgent questions but to try to save them up for the weekly meetings.

He said that the teams I was working with could probably answer work-related questions and that I should feel free to ask them directly.

That gave me the confidence to just go up to some of the senior members on the teams and ask them to explain things I didn't understand or things that had been discussed in meetings.

Luis was able to deal with his expectations of meeting frequently with his supervisor very professionally. He calmly explained what he wanted, and they were able to work out a solution that worked for both of them.

> TIP: Approaching someone, especially a supervisor, about something that's bothering you can be intimidating, but it is better than letting something go and having it build into a bigger problem over time. Speaking up politely and quietly in a private space usually gets the conversation started. And you get points for being mature.

***

Working Out Problems with Work

Generally, problems around internship work fall into three areas:

- Being left out of important project activities
- Too much boring grunt work and
- Work expectations.

Working Out Problems with Being Left Out

At times, interns can experience problems with being left out of the communications loop and important meetings and activities. Sometimes this is because the intern is not in attendance everyday and things move on without them. And sometimes it is just an oversight that can be remedied.

***

Michelle

After Michelle had been going to her internship for a few weeks, she began to get the feeling that she was going to be dealing with phones and paper and not people for the whole internship.

One day I came into the office at my usual time, and everyone involved in the events department was just leaving a meeting. I overheard them talking about a big wedding that had just been booked. One of the people handed me some papers and asked me to copy and distribute them to everyone. And I thought, "Did that just happen? Am I the copy clerk?" Luckily, I didn't say it. But I thought it. I was miserable for the rest of the day.

On the way home, I decided to make a list of what was making me mad, and I began to see that I was mad because I was being left out of the "real" work that the events team was doing. The next time I was at the internship, I had calmed down and didn't feel like I would start crying or say something stupid, and I told my supervisor that I would like to be more involved in the work of the events team and that I would be willing to adjust my schedule so that I wouldn't miss important meetings.

She said that was fine with her; she'd thought I didn't have any flexibility with my time.

Things got better from then on. I was often exhausted and worked way over the time I was supposed to be there, and even still did some grunt work, but I enjoyed every minute of it.

Identifying the problems and dealing with them calmly and professionally, like Michelle did, leads to a solution that works for everyone.

> **TIP:** If something doesn't feel right, something needs to be done. Sometimes you can fix things yourself. Often, just speaking up to the right person can start a discussion that can lead to a solution.

***

Usually interns are not intentionally left out of things. Projects just move along, and, unless you've made it a point to be included in all related communications and progress reports, you may miss some things. Having someone else on the team willing to forward information to you can also help with staying in the loop.

Working Out Problems with Too Much Grunt Work

Sometimes interns feel that they're getting all of the boring, routine jobs and none of the interesting work. But be careful about what you consider grunt work—there's a difference between work that's just meant to keep you busy, and necessary, routine tasks that are beneficial to the organization.

***

Jessica

Jessica was used to working at a fast pace, and when she had spent her first two weeks doing what she perceived was grunt work, she had had enough. She was about to march into her supervisor's office to demand that she be given more projects when she ran into a friend who had been an intern the previous semester.

The first thing my friend said after I ranted about my internship was, "You need to simmer down now."

She told me about all the boring work she had to do during her time as an intern and pointed out that I might need to step back and take a look at the big picture. She also pointed out that I had only been there for two weeks and that expecting to be head of a team was not realistic.

After I calmed down, I could see that she had a point. But I still wanted to do something more interesting and meaningful.

So eventually I sat down and listed all the things I had been doing and noted beside each item what I felt I had learned and how it contributed to the company's work. Then I listed some of the things I had seen other people doing and how I thought I could contribute to the teams or projects.

I also hauled out the original internship plan that we had discussed when I had my interview and highlighted some of the things

we had talked about. And then I scheduled a meeting with my super-
visor. I was calm by then, and we had a calm, productive meeting.

Luckily, Jessica took a deep breath and consulted a friend before she
marched into her supervisor's office to complain.

Tip: Complaining isn't so good. Neither is marching. Breathe
deeply, figure out what is really bothering you, and take the
time to come up with suggestions for solutions before meeting with
the person who can help with the problem.

***

There will always be misunderstandings and issues in any situation.
Learning how to handle them so they don't escalate into bigger problems is a skill worth practicing.

Working Out Problems with Work Expectations

There are sometimes problems around the work you're assigned at an
internship. For example, you might think deadlines are negotiable, like
some homework or papers, and your supervisor considers deadlines to
be drop-dead final. Or your supervisor is assigning you tasks that you
don't really like or don't think are helping you learn much. Or perhaps
the assignments aren't part of your original learning plan.

***

Alex
Alex had a bit of an adjustment period at his internship. He was used
to having a great deal of time being outdoors and active. Unfortunately,
this wasn't what the internship was turning out to be.

*After a few days my supervisor called me in and criticized me about
how long it took me to unpack and check in some orders. I was really
not too happy with that because I didn't think I would have to be
doing that kind of work when I signed on.*

> *The next day I was just about to quit, but some kids came in, and I started helping them and then took them out to demo some new equipment they were thinking of buying. My supervisor saw me outside and later called me in. He said he noticed I really worked well with the kids and told me they bought some of the things I had recommended.*
>
> *So I just decided to take a chance and tell him what I liked doing. . . . I said that I wanted to do the jobs he had given me, but I would also appreciate being able to spend more time with customers, especially outside with the equipment, since that was what I was really good at. He said I could do that, if I would help the other guys on the floor learn about the equipment and also still do some of the inventory work. I figured I could handle that, if I could get out more.*

Because he was able to identify what was bothering him and took a direct approach and talked with his supervisor Alex was able to find a win-win solution to his issue . . . always a better idea than quitting.

 TIP: Talking with the person who is in a position to make adjustments is a good way to finding a solution.

***

Working Out Problems with Juggling Responsibilities

Juggling refers to what happens when there are competing demands on your time. Internship. Classes. Work. Home life. Personal issues. Family. Social life. Some of your friends and colleagues, and especially your mentor, may be able to give you some hints about how handle all you have to do. But, basically, learning how to juggle and manage all you have to deal with is on you.

Dealing successfully with competing demands involves three main things:

- Prioritizing
- Time management and
- Saying no.

Juggling your responsibilities is something you'll probably have to do throughout your life, so it's good to start now.

Prioritizing

Sometimes it is difficult to sort out things that take precedence over others. Not everything can have the same importance in terms of the time you can give it. Work is pretty much right up there in importance, and at this point school and your internship are work. Anything that has a deadline moves up to the top of the list. Family obligations are also important.

Social and recreational activities and free time need to take a back seat right now. Some things get pushed off your plate entirely for the moment. You'll need to make the hard decision about what you can realistically fit into your daily schedule.

Time Management

Managing your time realistically is critical. Sit down, and list all that you have to accomplish, and figure out a workable schedule. Try to be realistic. Leaving your internship at 4:00 to pick up your younger brother across town at 4:15 is not realistic. Being at an internship function the evening before a big exam is not such a good idea, either.

It's always better to schedule in a little extra transition and travel time so that you aren't ending one appointment five minutes after you're due at another one. Things always take longer than you think, and you can always count on interruptions.

Saying No

You can't do everything, and the sooner you learn to pace yourself and begin to say, "I'm sorry, but I can't—I have a paper due/an appointment/a project due/a meeting/etc.," the sooner you'll feel the pressure letting up.

***

Luis
Luis is a prime example of someone who is juggling too much.

This has been a really tough few months. I've been in school, working part time, going to my volunteer job, and now my internship is taking up more and more of my time. I feel like I'm just spinning. . . . I've missed my weekly game of softball with my friends several times, and forget about having a social life.

When I was late for a client meeting at the internship to review a website design, I knew something had to go.

One of the guys I'd been working with told me I looked stressed out, and all I could do was say, "I'm more than stressed." Over lunch we started talking, and he told me he sometimes let himself get overscheduled and that I might just have to say no to some things for the time being.

Later I thought about what he said and realized that I got the internship I wanted and I really wanted to be successful there. School also had to be up there in my priorities, as did work, so it looked like the volunteer job and ball game would have to go temporarily. I didn't want to give up those things, but I just had to.

Luis was able to see that he simply couldn't do everything he wanted to do. He had to prioritize and let some things go for the time being.

Tip: Prioritizing and time management are two skills that most people have to constantly work on. It is too easy to want to do everything, but there are only so many hours in the day.

***

These juggling issues don't just crop up during internships, but often it is the first time that you'll become aware of them. It might be good to see how other people in your internship placement are juggling things or talk with people to see how they're managing. The more tips you get, the better you'll be able to handle all those competing demands.

FACING THE ISSUES AND WORKING THINGS OUT

The main thread running through this chapter is figuring out what the problem is and speaking up. Without doing those two things, you can't expect anything to change.

Identifying the Issues

The first step to finding a solution to any problem is identifying the issue. If you can't name the problem, how are you going to find a solution to it? Be very honest with yourself, and ask, "What did I expect? Am I being realistic given what I know about this business or organization now?"

Figure out what the problem is and what you hope will change. Can you suggest a solution? Can you suggest how a change will help you do your work better? Once you've targeted the issues that you feel you need to deal with, then it is time for the next step.

Speaking Up

The next step is to speak up. Don't be afraid to speak up. Speaking up in a calm, professional manner can head off many misunderstandings before they become problems. It's your responsibility as an independent learner and worker to identify and deal with things that are bothering you. No one else will do it for you.

GETTING BACK ON TRACK

You can work out some of the issues and problems yourself after some serious thought, but sometimes you'll need to talk with someone else. That someone else is your supervisor at work or your internship coordinator at your school. Or perhaps your mentor is the best person to help you work through things.

Many of these issues can be avoided by taking steps before you start your internship. If you and your supervisor agree on a learning plan or use the one provided by your school or your internship placement, then you have a document to refer to if things start to go off the rails.

Go back to your original learning plan agreed on, change some goals, talk with your mentor about making changes, or work on the goals from chapter 6.

You may feel like you've hit a brick wall when you realize things are not perfect and that something needs to change. However, part of learning at an internship involves identifying problems and challenges and figuring out how to deal with them.

It's important to remember to always maintain your professionalism and always work to find ways to solve the problems that work for both you and your supervisor.

IT WON'T LAST FOREVER

When you think about it, an internship takes up a pretty small portion of your life—probably only a few months. Keep the time in mind as you negotiate your way through some of the problems and issues. You can learn just as much from a negative experience as you can from a positive one. For the time being, take it one day at a time, and do your best. When you look back on this experience, you may forget some of the struggles, but hopefully you'll have learned from them.

Once you've been able to identify the problematic issues you're facing and have dealt with them in a professional and mature manner, you'll again be excited about your internship experience and will move into feeling a sense of accomplishment and independence.

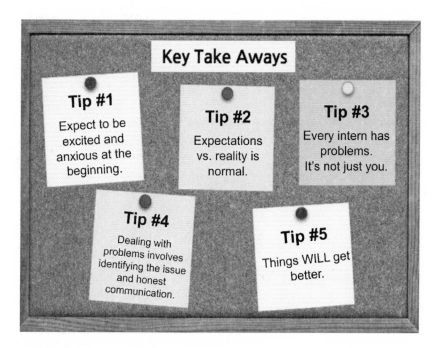

Key Take Aways

Tip #1
Expect to be excited and anxious at the beginning.

Tip #2
Expectations vs. reality is normal.

Tip #3
Every intern has problems. It's not just you.

Tip #4
Dealing with problems involves identifying the issue and honest communication.

Tip #5
Things WILL get better.

8

Finish Strong

You've almost completed your internship, and you may be wondering, was it all worth it? What did you really learn? This is the time to take stock of your experience and think about how you felt at the start, the ups and downs, what you learned, how you feel now, and even perhaps how you've changed.

You made it through some wobbly periods plus some great successes. You gained confidence in your ability to overcome obstacles in a professional manner; you're feeling pretty good. And you may have even asked for more challenging assignments and for more time and attention from your supervisor.

***

Alex
Alex noticed that customers were beginning to ask for his help. His supervisor commented that this was because he had been able to work so well with them and was patient when showing them how to keep their equipment in good shape.

> *This group of kids from the middle school had been bringing their boards in individually for the last month or so, and one day they all came in together and just hung around while I fixed some things for them. They said they were forming a skateboarding team and wondered if I would help them learn how to keep their boards in good shape themselves. I said sure . . . they were nice little dudes.*

> *When my supervisor heard us talking, he suggested that the store*
> *give them a few inexpensive things for free, like stickers and posters*
> *and stuff, and maybe we could be one of their sponsors, for good*
> *PR. That sounded great. I liked working with the kids, and the store*
> *would be getting something out of it, too.*

Alex felt great that he was asked by the skateboarding team to help out. He also felt that he was being treated as an adult by his supervisor, who offered to get the team some free materials and even get the store to become a sponsor because of his involvement. Plus, it didn't hurt that his supervisor had something positive to say about him.

After all the ups and downs of Alex's internship, he now was beginning to see what he had accomplished.

 TIP: Feel proud about what you've accomplished in your internship. You worked hard.

***

BUT WHAT SKILLS DID YOU REALLY LEARN?

You learned some great skills that you can use. You can probably think about these skills in two ways: First, you learned some job-related skills. And, second, you learned some life skills.

Job-Related Skills

Job-related skills are skills you learned that were specific to your job.

***

Michelle

When Michelle thought about what she learned in her internship, she realized that she learned new skills specific to her work.

> *I was surprised to see that I learned a bunch of new things. I learned*
> *how to do a PowerPoint presentation to clients, and I learned how*

to use Microsoft Project, a program in project management for events. I knew a little about Excel, but now I can really use it. And, of course, I learned how to use the hotel's reservation system.

Michelle started her internship working on the hotel desk where she learned the reservation system. When she began working with the events team, she learned to use both Excel and Microsoft Project for project management. In addition, Michelle learned how to use Power-Point for client presentations.

***
***

Luis
Luis, too, was surprised about what job-related skills he learned.

Yeah. I thought I knew most of the programs I needed in Web design but found there were lots more programs that are used especially when working on client projects. I finally learned about all there is to know about WordPress. The company uses this a lot with clients, and now I'm very comfortable with it.
I learned more about computer coding that I know I can use in the future. And I learned how to make a presentation to clients without using all that computer jargon.

Luis was able to expand his technical skills especially in upgrading his WordPress and coding abilities. Above all, he learned how to present to clients using everyday language and not computerspeak.

***
***

Alex
Alex wasn't 100 percent happy with his internship at the sports retailer. At first he thought he did not learn much, but when asked to list the things he did, he was surprised at what he learned.

Okay, I guess I did learn some stuff. I learned all about logistics management. That's a fancy way of saying that I tracked orders from suppliers and checked them as they came in. I also got back to the supplier when stuff wasn't right. I learned a lot about maintaining and repairing sports equipment other than skateboards. And, yeah, I learned how give advice to customers about what equipment they needed.

Alex was surprised to have learned the basics of logistics management and his ability to do detailed follow-up. He also learned more about maintaining and repairing sports equipment and how to listen and give advice to customers.

***
***

Jessica

Jessica wanted to learn as much as she could in her internship in cybersecurity

I was so excited about this internship because it is in a field I really wanted to learn more about. The company where I interned focused on digital forensics—you know, getting at information from a computer that the user thought was hidden. I learned two really important skills in my internship: First, was how to get at information that was hidden or erased from a computer. And second, how to explain what I was doing in non–computer talk so that anyone would understand it.

Jessica's focus was on learning more about computer systems in cybersecurity. She learned how to find information on a computer that was thought lost. And she learned how to explain what she did in non-computerspeak so that others could easily understand it.

> **Tip:** You can see that these skills are specific to an industry or work area. Take the time to list the specific skills you learned. Think about what you now know that you did not know when you started your internship.

***

Life Skills

You learned and strengthened some life skills. These are the skills that you can use in any career or industry. You already started to think about some of these skills when you prepared for your interview. These are the skills that employers, no matter the field, want to see. They include:

- Work ethic
- Teamwork and
- Communication.

Think about the examples of these skills that you prepared for your interview. You probably used examples from your school, college, or some past part-time work. Now you can find examples from your internship that will show what you learned. These examples would show how you:

- Met a deadline
- Set and achieved goals
- Worked in a team
- Helped out another team member
- Talked in front of a group
- Worked on a project with your colleagues
- Discussed a situation with you supervisor or
- Helped solve a customer's problem.

 Tip: You'll have many examples of these life skills to show. Take the time now to identify them.

Other Life Skills

Two other areas that are important are:

- Planning and organizing and
- Personal awareness.

These are two areas that are also important to employers and college-admissions counselors. Employers and counselors want to know how well you manage your time and if you realize what you've learned from your experiences.

Planning and organizing means that you're able to:

- Schedule your time effectively
- Think ahead and make plans to achieve your objectives
- Set priorities and
- Use tools, like a checklist, to track your progress.

During a job or college interview, regarding your planning and organizing skills, you may be asked to *Describe a time when you had to prepare in advance for a meeting. What did you do? What was the outcome? What, if anything, could you have done to prepare better?*

***

Luis
In Luis's internship, he was part of a weekly client meeting. He was able to give this example.

> *I had an internship at City Net Design. Each Monday afternoon the client team met to discuss progress on the client's project. One Thursday afternoon the team leader asked me prepare a list of activities we had already done for this client for the Monday meeting. It was late on Thursday, and I had a sports team event that night and some other things to do over the weekend. So I decided to come in early on Monday and do the list using our client files.*
>
> *In the end it worked out okay. I got the list done for the meeting. But I missed out on an important meeting about a new client on Monday morning because I had to complete the list. Next time, I think I would find some way to do some work on Friday so that I don't miss out on other things going on in the office.*

In his example Luis was able to show that he did plan how and when to do the client list. But he chose to wait until Monday to do it and missed out on an important meeting. When next asked to do a task for the team, he learned that he should not leave it until the last moment.

Tip: When you give an example of what you've done, be sure to show what you learned from the experience.

***

Another area of importance to organizations and colleges is your personal awareness.

Personal awareness means that you:

* Look for ways to learn more about yourself
* Are open to new ideas
* Accept feedback and look for ways to improve
* Understand own impact on others and
* Show an awareness of own emotions.

About personal awareness you may be asked to *Tell me about a time when you had to change your thinking about an issue. Why did you have to change your mind? What did you do? What did you learn from this situation?*

***

Michelle
In Michelle's internship she had to work through a problem that she thought she knew the answer to.

In my internship at the Lakeview Hotel, I was part of the events team. We wanted to find a way to make sure that everything that needed to be done for an event was completed beforehand. I was asked to develop a checklist to make sure everything was done on time. I was excited because I knew I could do this. So I used an Excel spreadsheet and listed all the activities. I did one spreadsheet for weddings and one for conferences.

When I presented it, the team found activities that I had left off and ones that were in the wrong order. I thought I had included everything in the right order. I was asked to include the team's feedback and revise the checklist. Next time I'll not just jump in and think I know everything. I'll talk to the other team members as I work to get their input.

In her example, Michelle showed that she has learned to get input from other team members when doing an activity that affects them all. This insight will help her be a better team member in work or college.

 TIP: Be sure to show how you include feedback from your colleagues in your examples.

***

***

Alex

Alex began his internship not knowing what he wanted to do. But his experience gave him insight into what he wanted to do in the future.

When I started my internship at the sports store, I didn't know what I wanted. I just thought I would get to see all the new skateboarding equipment and some other sports equipment. But I really didn't like working in a store so much. The best thing about my internship was when I was able to advise people on different equipment.

I really liked talking with middle school kids about skateboarding and other sports and helping them to learn more about what they need. I really would like to work more with these kids.

Alex was surprised about how much he liked helping others who wanted to do different sports. His internship experience has opened some new doors that could lead to coaching kids or working with sports groups.

***

 TIP: Give examples of how your experience in your internship changed your thinking.

Remember, your examples for planning and organizing and personal awareness don't have to be perfect, but they need to be your real experiences.

SHOW WHAT YOU LEARNED

It's great to list the job-related and life skills you've learned. But any future employer or college-admissions counselor will want to know if you can show evidence or give real examples of these skills.

There are three ways to show what you've learned:

1. Your updated résumé
2. Your transcript and
3. Solid examples of your skills for job and college interviews and applications.

Update Your Résumé

After you've completed your internship, be sure to add your experience to your résumé. This does not have to be a long statement, but it should summarize your experience and show the skills you now have.

***

Michelle

After Michelle completed her internship with a hotel, she included her experience on her résumé:

- Assisted hotel staff in day-to-day activities, including reservations, office work, and customer service
- Participated in team meetings to plan and organize conferences and weddings
- Used Excel spreadsheet and Microsoft Project to list specific steps for each event and developed a checklist to ensure that all steps were completed
- Prepared PowerPoint presentations for customers
- Summarized customer-feedback forms for management

Michelle was able to show that she has job-related skills (reservation system, Microsoft Project, and Excel spreadsheet) and life skills (planning and organizing under a deadline, teamwork, and customer service).

***

***

Luis

After Luis's internship he included his experience on his résumé:

As part of the client-accounts team at City Net Design

- Participated in weekly team meetings reviewing client projects
- Designed social-media platform for professional law firm incorporating client feedback
- Designed website using WordPress for new restaurant with input from client
- Increased knowledge of computer coding
- Used PowerPoint to present to clients
- Summarized all activities done for current client base

Luis was able to show that he used his technical knowledge and skills to contribute to client projects. He also showed that he was a team player in a professional organization.

***

***

Alex

Alex's internship experience included the following:

- Assisted customers in a sports store in purchasing equipment
- Listened to customers and advised on technical aspects of equipment
- Met with middle school skateboarding club to help them keep their boards in good condition
- Maintained and repaired various sports equipment
- Tracked and checked incoming orders from suppliers to make sure they were correct
- Followed up on any wrong orders with suppliers

Alex was able to show that he gained customer-service experience but also handled details regarding orders. He also learned how to interface with suppliers and follow up on missing orders. He learned to work with groups of young teenagers, passing on his enthusiasm about skateboarding.

Although Alex did not like working in retail, he showed that he gained both job-related skills and life skills.

***

***

Jessica

Jessica was sometimes so focused on learning more advanced computer skills she almost forgot to include what other skills she leaned on her résumé.

As part the forensics cyber team at Internet Secure

- Tracked Internet usage of restricted programs for a client company using I Track
- Retrieved lost information from a computer
- Presented findings to team and client using layman's language
- Wrote formal reports for court submissions
- Attended training sessions in digital-media analysis

Jessica learned some advanced computer skills. And she presented her findings to the team and clients using everyday language. She also had experience in writing formal reports that were used in court.

***

> **Tip:** When you write up your internship experience for your résumé, be sure to include both your job-related skills and your life skills.

Write a Description for your Transcript

***

Michelle

Your school or college may ask you for a summary of your internship that can be attached to your transcript. Michelle's transcript summarized her internship experience.

Michelle Reddington
Internship Transcript Summary

For five months during my senior year in high school I interned at the Lakeview Hotel and Conference Center. The hotel specializes in business conferences and weddings. I interned with the staff team that planned and organized conferences and weddings.

It was my function to help plan the conferences and weddings by ensuring that all the details needed to make the conference or wedding a success were completed. I learned to use an Excel spreadsheet and Microsoft Project to list what needed to be done for each event. I also helped to develop a checklist so that each team member would know that the steps were completed.

Whenever possible, I attended the conference or wedding to help ensure its smooth running. I was the liaison between the hotel and the individual guests and handled specific requests or problems.

As a result of my internship experience, I have strengthened my time management skills as I learned the critical importance of meeting deadlines to ensure a successful event. I also learned the importance of being an active member of a team and of communicating with team members. My computer skills have increased as a result of my job responsibilities. I also learned how good customer service is critical for a successful event.

 TIP: Writing a description for your transcript will help you organize you thoughts and identify what you've learned.

***

Give Real-Life Examples

Even if a future employer or college-admissions counselor has read your résumé and transcript, they would, more than likely, want to know some more information about your skills. Think about the questions that an interviewer might have asked when you applied for you internship. Remember that the three skills that most employers are looking for in candidates (and we know you're probably sick of hearing about them) are:

- Work ethic
- Teamwork and
- Communication.

And, in addition, don't forget the two other areas of interest to employers and college-admissions counselors:

- Planning and organizing and
- Personal awareness.

Every internship is different, so there is no one way to show these skills. But if you think about what you did in your internship, you can be sure that you'll find examples of how you demonstrated these skills.

Make a list of the examples that you would use to show these skills now while the experience of your internship is fresh.

Tip: If you take the time to get your internship experience summarized for your résumé and transcript and you think about how to use your experience to give some real-world examples of what you've done, you're well on the way to getting the most out of your experience.

USE YOUR INTERNSHIP LEARNING FOREVER

It's hard to believe that this experience of a few months of your life can be so important. But it is something that you'll always remember.

Many people who do an internship as part of their time in school or on their own talk about that experience many years into the future.

***

Michelle
Michelle interviewed her manager for her career-path project, and she learned that her manager had done an internship.

When I interviewed my manager for my career-path project, I was surprised to learn that she had done an internship. She had completed an internship in accounting when she was in college. Her internship was in the accounts department of a large hotel, but she learned that she preferred to be out front, working with people, rather than in the back office.

She completed her bachelor's degree in accounting, but she took a number of electives in hospitality and management and found her first job as a reception-desk supervisor in a hotel. It was interesting to hear that my manager credits her internship with helping her decide on the right career path.

When Michelle interviewed her manager, she was able to see just how important an internship experience can be. She really got a different perspective on her experience than she had just looking at her day-to-day routine.

Tip: Your internship experience will be with you forever. Whether your experience helps you to decide on a career path, choose a college major, or show you what you really don't want to do, it will help you make the right decisions for your future.

***

KEEP A RECORD

To get the most out of your experience, you should find a way to keep a record of your internship. You'll build on and strengthen the skills you learned in your internship as you go forward in your career and college. Don't forget them. Use them as examples of your learning in your future job and college interviews.

One good way to keep a record of your learning is to create a portfolio. Keep a record of the work you've done. This can include:

- Specific projects assigned to you by your supervisor or manager
- Projects for your school or college, including the career-path interview with your manager or supervisor, the organizational structure, or a list of jargon or vocabulary related to your internship field
- A record of the articles you read in magazines, newspapers, or online related to your internship field
- Job-related skills you learned
- Life skills you strengthened
- A record of how you answered possible interview questions in your interview preparation
- Any blogs or Internet postings you did related to your internship
- Your elevator speech (updated)
- What your learned (what you know now that you did not know before you did your internship)
- Some journal entries
- An updated résumé and
- Your transcript entry.

Setting up a portfolio does two things for you: First, it pulls together what you've done and learned in one place so you can refer back to it. Second, it is a well-organized record of your experience that might be of interest to your interviewer in your next job or college interview.

 TIP: Start your portfolio when you begin your internship so that you have all your material and notes together.

IT'S NOT OVER YET

Now that you've updated your résumé and transcript and thought about the skills you learned in your internship, there are a few more things you need to do so that you get the most mileage from your experience.

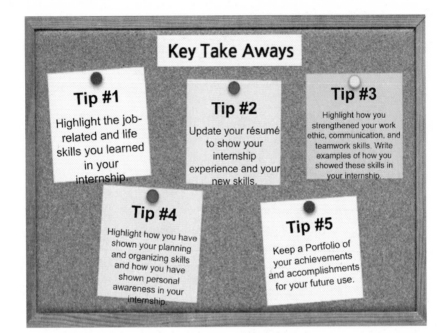

⑨

Wind Down and Say Goodbye

Not long after you finally feel settled into the workplace, you realize that the internship will be over in a matter of weeks. That is the nature of internships. You're finally having success, and now you have to start thinking about leaving!

SAYING GOODBYE

Sometimes it can be tough to wrap up projects and say goodbye to clients and coworkers. You probably think that this should be the easiest part of the internship experience, but it isn't so.

You're nearing the end of your experience and should be very proud of what you've achieved, but sometime endings can be very difficult.

Don't Slam the Door!

Don't shoot yourself in the foot as your internship winds down. Now is the time to practice how to end an important activity or experience gracefully and professionally.

Some people can't leave or end anything without slamming a door. Others pull in and avoid their feelings. Some interns decide that the best way to deal with their confusing feelings is to joke around and pretend that none of it mattered anyway. They begin to unravel all of what they have accomplished.

Be aware of how important the final weeks are. Keep showing up on time and doing your best work. People will remember you mostly from your last weeks as an intern. They'll forget the time you jammed the copy machine. They'll forget about the time you were listing all the things you'd change about the company while the CEO was standing right behind you. But they *will* remember how nice it was to receive thank-you notes from you—notes that mentioned how you appreciated all of the help they gave you during your time there.

***

Alex

Alex had some good experiences at his internship, and he learned a great deal. However, he continued to have some negative experiences with his supervisor. He had decided to stick it out because his guidance counselor pointed out that the internship wasn't going to last forever.

When I realized I only had a week left until the internship was over, I was really happy. But I also felt sad, since most of the people there had been really nice to me and had spent time helping me, especially at the beginning. I did have an interview with my supervisor, and he was still not so great to talk to, but he did go over the things I had done, and he seemed pretty okay with me . . . At least he didn't give me a list of things that he thought were wrong. And he also said he hoped I would continue with the group of middle school kids, since I seemed to do really well with them and they all seemed to really like me.

I felt kind of proud that he had noticed that they like me as much as I like them. So I guess I'll write him a thank-you note like my counselor says I should do, and I'll ask him to be a reference now that I know he doesn't think I was a totally lousy intern.

Alex was surprised to learn that his supervisor actually valued his contributions and had noticed him. He hadn't just been looking to criticize the way Alex chose to do some of his work.

Alex could have unraveled all of his hard work by not being professional and not having an exit interview. He could have just left on the last day without a proper goodbye. He could have forgotten all about writing thank-you notes. But he didn't. He stuck it out and ended his internship on a positive note.

 TIP: Even though the internship might not have been all you had hoped for, take the best from it, and leave the right way.

***

As your internship comes to an end, give yourself time to enjoy your successes and accomplishments. Don't be afraid to tell people that you'll miss working with them and how much you enjoyed your experience. They're probably not so happy about your leaving either. And they might be happy to know they were appreciated and will be missed.

Tie Up Loose Ends

If you're working on a project that extends past your last day, go the extra mile and create a status report of where you're leaving it. Your supervisor and team will be thankful that you're not leaving them to figure out what parts of the project are missing.

***

Michelle

Michelle would be leaving her internship before the event she was working on took place.

I was really upset when I realized the big wedding I was working on would take place three weeks after I finished my internship. My supervisor knew this too, and the team was not happy I'd be leaving before we completed the task, so we talked and worked it out so that I could continue to come in to work on the wedding and attend with the others on the team to make sure the event went off as we were planning.

She even said she would try to arrange for me to get a stipend for the time that I worked. That was really a nice surprise. It's exciting to think that I'll get to see the big wedding that I've been working on all these months.

Michelle was happy that she could see her project through to the end. The wedding couple was also pleased, because they had liked working with her over the past months.

> **TIP:** Just because your internship is ending doesn't mean your relationship with the people there has to end. Coworkers and clients are happy when an intern keeps in touch or finishes up a project. If you've been dealing with clients, let them know when you'll be leaving so they don't just find you gone one day.

***

***

Luis

Luis found it hard to leave his internship at the end, since one of his projects was not quite finished. He had finished his part in other websites, but this one was really important to him.

I grew to like the people at the organization I was building the website for, and leaving them before the project was finished made me really sad.

I told them way ahead of time that I would be finishing my internship before the project was completed, and they understood . . . but I was still upset. I reassured them that I would leave notes and any other important information for the rest of the team about what we had discussed and decided about their Web design so that there would be no interruption of the building of their website. I think they understood, but, still, it was really hard for me. This situation also made me see how important it is to write down things and keep really accurate notes so that others can step in and understand what is going on with a project.

Luis was able to reassure his clients that their project would continue on schedule and that he would make sure of that.

> **Tip:** Leave notes for anything that needs follow-up. Make sure the right person has all of your information and notes regarding what you worked on.

***

Make an Appointment with Your Supervisor

At least a week before your last day, make an appointment with your supervisor to thank him once again for the help and guidance he provided. Use this appointment to conduct an informal assessment of how you performed on the job.

Your placement may have an actual exit interview, which should give you a great deal of feedback about your experience in that business or organization. If there is no formal exit interview, these are some questions you might want to ask:

- What were my strongest areas?
- Did I meet your expectations? Why or why not?
- What could I have done better?
- What advice can you give me based on my work here?
- Is there anyone else you think I should speak with?

AFTER THE INTERNSHIP IS OVER

Hopefully your internship was a great experience for you. You learned a lot and perhaps have been able to make some decisions.

Before you move on to other things—hold on. There are still some things that need to be done.

Make Sure Your Résumé is Updated

If you haven't already updated your résumé, make sure you do that before you forget important things.

An internship can be the beginning of a career path. You'll be missing a great opportunity if you look at it as just an isolated experience.

Keep your internship experience up to date—both in your mind *and* on your résumé. Refer back to your journal or blogs to help yourself remember the ups and downs and all of the things you learned during this exciting period. Even if you didn't really like your internship, you can still get mileage out of it.

You can see the updated résumés of Michelle, Alex, Luis, and Jessica at the end of this chapter in EXTRA INFO 9A.

Send Thank-You Notes (or E-mails If Your Internship Was Really Casual)

Write to your main internship supervisor and mentor, as well as to anyone else you worked with frequently. Thank them for making the internship a positive experience, and tell them what you learned as a result. Even if you hated the experience and have no interest in pursuing either that organization or that field, you still need to write a brief, polite thank-you note.

Also, write brief notes to anyone else in the organization with whom you interacted. They could be valuable contacts in the future, and you'll want to maintain a connection with them. A canned verbal thank-you isn't enough. Handwritten notes are best.

***

Jessica

Even though I had been through this before at my previous internship and sort of knew what to expect, I was super sad when this one was over. The people I worked with had been so nice to me, and I can't believe how much new stuff I learned. If I hadn't done this internship I might have not been sure about concentrating on cybercrime in school. I bought a box of note cards and wrote a thank-you note to everyone. I wanted to let them know how much I appreciated their help and how much like a regular team member they had made me feel. I also want to keep them as close friends and colleagues in the future because they know so much and

I know I'll be able to ask them for advice and recommendations after I graduate.

***

Request Letters of Recommendation

Request a letter (or letters) of recommendation. You could do this in your thank-you note or in a note sent a few weeks later. Make the process easy for the writer by giving a list of points they might include in the letter—such as your basic job duties, what you learned, and how you excelled. The reflecting you've already done will help you prepare for requesting these letters. You should try to get letters of recommendation to keep on hand from the people you worked with while your time with them is fresh in their minds. But, also, ask if you might use them as references in the future.

If You Didn't Have a Great Experience, Take the High Road

Unfortunately, not all internships are spectacular. Even if you didn't have the internship you expected, you can still benefit from your experience.

If you didn't like the internship experience or career area, meet with a career counselor to discuss alternative areas in another field, but make sure it was the career area you didn't like and not just that particular internship site.

Make Sure Your School Has What it Needs

If the school program has an official evaluation form, make sure you hand it in to the correct person, and, if necessary have your supervisor fill out his section. Even if you complete a report, most schools will not award credit until they have all the required documents in your file. Make sure any other paperwork your school needs is completed as quickly as possible. Check with the internship coordinator to make sure things are complete.

Don't Lose Touch

Your internship experience can be the start of building your network, which will eventually be essential in building your career. Everyone you met or worked with during your internship is a potential connection for another internship, job opening, or professional-development opportunity. Stay in touch with your fellow interns, coworkers, supervisor, and, especially, mentor by connecting with them on social-media sites.

For instance, you could send your previous internship mentor an e-mail if you see the company has been in the news, or you could check in with a former coworker to see how things are going since you left. Once you get on LinkedIn, you can stay in touch that way, but be careful about asking to link with people higher up on the professional ladder than you if you don't really know them well.

And while you're keeping in touch with former colleagues, try to keep in touch with how you've changed as a result of your internship. Take time to be proud of your accomplishments. Think about your new levels of self-confidence and self-esteem. Use your recent experience in the real world to guide your thinking about future plans and possibilities.

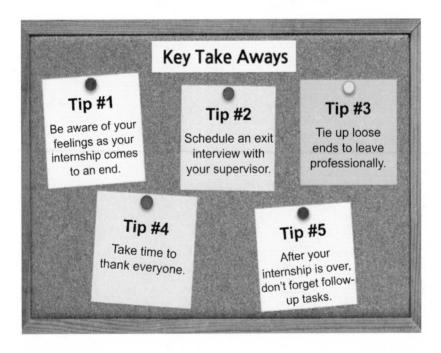

Key Take Aways

Tip #1
Be aware of your feelings as your internship comes to an end.

Tip #2
Schedule an exit interview with your supervisor.

Tip #3
Tie up loose ends to leave professionally.

Tip #4
Take time to thank everyone.

Tip #5
After your internship is over, don't forget follow-up tasks.

EXTRA INFO 9A: Students' Updated Résumés

Michelle Reddington

6 Pine Street ■ Centertown, CA
222.222.2222
mredddington@email.com

EDCATION: Centertown High School. Expected graduation — June (date)

WORK EXPERIENCE: ← | Internship and new computer program experience added to resume.

Events Team Intern (date) — (date)
Lakeview Hotel and Conference Center, Centertown, CA

- Assisted hotel staff in day-to-day activities including reservations, office work and customer service.
- Participated in team meetings to plan and organize conferences and weddings.
- Used Excel spreadsheet and Microsoft Projects to list specific steps for each event and developed a checklist to ensure that all steps were completed.
- Prepared and delivered Power Point presentation to customers.
- Summarized customer feedback forms for management.

Child Care Provider (date) — Present
- Provide child care for several families weekends and during school vacations

COMPUTER SKILLS Proficient with
- Microsoft Projects ←
- Microsoft Word, Excel, and PowerPoint
- Online Database Research, and
- Basic Wix Web Design

VOLUNTEER EXPERIENCE
- Big Brother / Big Sisters — Homework Helper
- Centertown Public Library
- High School fundraising team to aid the homeless food
- Town food pantry, collecting, stocking, outreach

ACHIEVEMENTS
- National Honor Society: (date) — Present
- Academic Honor Roll: (date) — Present
- Student Government, Secretary (date — Present)

INTERESTS / ACTIVITIES
- Member of Centertown High School Cross Country Team
- Year Book Production Committee
- Girl Scouts

| Internship supervisor is an additional reference. |

References:

Mr. Seth Smith, English Teacher	Ms. M.L. Jones, Librarian	*Ms. Jane Simmons*
Centertown High School	Centertown Public Library	*Manager, Lakeville Hotel*
(Work) 555.555.5555	(Work) 555.555.5555	*(Work) 555.555.5555*
E-mail: ssmith1@email.com	E-mail: mljones@email.com	E-mail: jsimmons@email.com

Alex Boyd
10 Cedar Street, Place, FL 12345
566.555.2222 ■ E-mail: aboyd@email.net

> Internship and new computer program experience added to resume.

EDUCATION   Central High School, Place, FL
Graduation Anticipated (Date)

WORK EXPERIENCE

Southeastern Sports, Place, FL — Intern *(dates)*

- Assisted customers in a sports store equipment department
- Consulted with customers and advised on technical aspects of equipment
- Demonstrated various sports equipment for customers
- Worked with middle school skateboarding team to advise on equipment upkeep and maintenance and safety
- Maintained and repaired various sports equipment
- Tracked and checked incoming orders using inventory management program
- Followed up on orders with supplier errors

Franklin Auto Service, Place, FL (Date) to Present

- Assist family business to provide detailing service to customer's automobiles
- Create and distribute 200 flyers about Detailing service
- Help collate invoices for monthly billing and enter payments into Quicken software

Pet Sitter (Date) - Present

- Provide pet sitting services including dog walking, feeding and mail pick up to neighborhood homes

INTERESTS / ACTIVITIES

- Member of Central High School Drama Club – Stage Crew
- Designed and built skateboard for Career and Technology Fair

COMPUTER SKILLS
- Quick Books Inventory Management
- Proficient with Microsoft Word, Excel, Internet, Social Media, Quicken

> Internship supervisor is an additional reference.

References:

Mr. James Wyatt, CTE Teacher
Central High School
566.486.2222
E-mail: jwyatt@email.net

Mr. John W. Greene
Manager, Southeastern Sports
555-555-5555
E-mail: jwgreene@email.org

Jessica Davison

6 Elm Avenue
Willington, MD 12345
766.444.4444 ■ jdavison1234@email.com

EDUCATION

Willington County Community College — Homeland Security Criminal Justice Institute Program.
Currently enrolled with concentration in Cybercrime
Relevant Courses: Introduction to the Criminal Justice System; Criminal Law; Overview of
Cybercrime; Computer Forensics I

Willington High School, Willington, MD - High School Diploma (Date)

> Internship and
> computer experience
> added to Jessica's
> resume.

WORK EXPERIENCE

Internet Secure, Willington, MD — Intern (dates)

As part the cyber forensics team
- Tracked internet usage of restricted programs for client companies using ITRAK
- Retrieved lost information from computers
- Presented findings to team and client using layman's language
- Wrote formal reports for court submissions
- Attended training sessions in Digital Media analysis

Willington Police Department — Intern (Dates)
- Participated in 8 week training for local police departments in Department of Justice
  Cybercrimes Training
- Participated in cases involving detective and forensic units, court appearances, case follow-up
- Participated in sit-alongs, ride-alongs with detectives and patrolmen

Super Snacks – Scooper (Dates)
- Provided friendly customer service in small family ice-cream/organic snack store
- Handled cash and credit card transactions and balanced out register nightly
- Monitored inventory ad assisted with reordering inventory

Sam's Subs – Counter (Dates)
- Restocked condiments, napkins and maintained a clean counter.
- Provided great customer service for walk-in customers on each shift.
- Operated cash register, POS, and frequent guest card system.

COMPUTER SKILLS Proficient with

- ITRAK usage tracking program
- Microsoft Word, Excel, and PowerPoint
- Internet Research, online database research
- Installing/uninstalling computer software
- Checking computers for virus and other
  malware.

VOLUNTEER EXPERIENCE

- **Willington Toys for Tots Drive** — Head of area collection team
  past four years
- **Library** — Homework Helpers Reading Program past two years
- **Police Athletic League** —
  Active with all summer
  activities for past three years

INTERESTS
Community Basketball Team; Race for the Cure - Helped with organization and set up and ran with local Police Athletic League (PAL) team.

References

John D. White
Manager, Internet Secure, Internship Supervisor
555-555-5555

Sergeant Jack McDell, PAL Coordinator
Willington Police Department
555-555-5555

Captain Carolyn Smith
Willington Police Department
555-555-5555

Marissa Kennely, Owner
Super Snacks
444-444-44

Internship supervisor is an
additional reference

luis belen

295 Main Avenue • East, IL • 12345
(555) 123-7654 • E-MAIL lbelen@email.com

Internship experience
and new computer
skills added to Luis'
resume.

EDUCATION

East Community College, East Campus, East IL
Anticipate **AS degree**, Web Design, June (date)
Honor roll each quarter

East High School, East, IL Graduated (date)
Yearbook Committee, Intramural Volleyball

**WORK
EXPERIENCE**

City Net Design, East, IL — Intern (dates)
As part of the client Accounts team in City Net Design
  • Participated in weekly team meetings reviewing client projects
  • Designed social media platform for law firm incorporating client feedback
  • Designed website using Word Press for new restaurant with input from
    client
  • Increased knowledge of computer coding
  • Used Power Point to present plans to clients
  • Summarized all activities done for current client base

Panera - September (date) - Present
  • Lead Set-up team to organize coffee and soft drinks service area for
    each shift

McDonalds (Dates)
  • Customer Service order taking and filling

ABC Supermarket – Night Shift (Dates)
  • Team member responsible for inventory and shelf stacking

**COMPUTER
SKILLS**

Extensive use of current industry standard web design programs such as
  • Word Press, Dreamweaver, Flux
  • Photoshop
  • Muse
  • Power Point
  • Excel
  • Microsoft Word

**VOLUNTEER
EXPERIENCE**

Tutor, Adams Settlement House (dates)
  • Helped elementary school students with homework assignments
  • Served snacks and helped students with clean up
  • Participated in afterschool recreation activities

Soup Kitchen Server, Adams Settlement House (dates)
  • Served holiday meals to homeless and other less fortunate community
    members
  • Helped with set up and clean up

References:

Mr. Steve Smith, Creative Director	Ms. Gloria Markham,	Mr. Ben White,
City Net Design, East, IL	Academic Advisor	Manager
Work: 555-555-5555	East Community College	Panera
SSmith@citygraphics.com	Work: 555-543-6543	Work: 555-543-6543
	Gmarkham@email.edu	bwhite1@gmail.com

Internship supervisor is
an added reference.

10

New Beginnings

You did it! You finished your internship. You worked through the ups and downs, and you built and strengthened the skills and attitudes you need for your future. It's time now to think about what you want to do next.

MAKE THE RIGHT DECISIONS FOR YOUR FUTURE

You may be surprised to see just what part your internship plays in your decision making about your future. And these decisions may be about what you'll do next semester as well as what you want to do in the longer term.

***

Michelle

When Michelle took on her internship, she thought that it would just be an interesting experience. But she soon found that the experience was becoming a big part of her thoughts about her future.

I decided on my internship because it was something different. Everyone, it seems, was pushing me to go to a four-year college and to get involved in teaching or social work. The internship at the conference center was in business, and so I thought I would give it a try. And it has really made a difference to me.

Now when I talk with my guidance counselor, she is no longer pushing me but asking what I am interested in and what I want to do. I think she is really hearing me now.

I decided to go to the local community college after graduation and get my associate's degree in business. I loved the hospitality sector of my internship but want to have more opportunities than just hotel or conference work. I will probably then continue on to a four-year college. My younger sisters won't need me around so much, and my mom thinks we can do it financially, even if I go away.

So, all in all, my internship has really made a difference in my life.

Michelle found that her internship had really helped her to mature so that she could have a clear focus on her future and not feel so pushed around by others. She decided on a business major in order to have some different options after graduation, and she has taken a realistic approach to getting her associate's and bachelor's degrees.

***

***

Alex

Alex, too, found that his internship experience has helped him make some decisions about his future.

Okay, I know that I really didn't like a lot about my internship, but there was a lot I did like. I got to know much more about sports equipment and met some great guys in different sporting clubs. And I really liked working with those middle school kids. And it was good that my guidance counselor was around to help me when things got a little rough.

So I decided that I wanted to do something with sports in the future. My guidance counselor got me to look at the community college that has a degree in recreation leadership and outdoor activities. And that sounded great for me.

I'm now volunteering with the middle school skateboarding team and have already joined the college's cycle team. I decided to work more hours for my uncle this summer and earn some money so I can buy a new bike.

I'll start college in the fall. So, yeah, I guess I wouldn't be going to college if I hadn't done that internship.

Alex stuck with his internship and was able to find a way to turn his passion for sports into a possible career. He found that he really liked working with younger kids and decided that his future will include sports leadership.

***
***

Luis
Luis knew from the start exactly what he wanted to get from his internship.

I wanted an internship where I could work with clients, and I was lucky to find exactly what I wanted. I not only learned how to deal with clients—and, yeah, some of them can be a real pain—but I even learned more Web-designing skills. I really would have liked to stay on with this company, but that was not going to be possible.

I graduate in June with my AS degree and will start job hunting. I have some great leads from the guys at the company. And I also picked up some freelance Web-design work. And that sure pays more than working at McDonald's.

I know I'm in a competitive field, but I feel confident that I'll find the right job for me. I guess my experience in a real business has given me more confidence in my skills. I know that I wouldn't feel so good about my technical skills and my client skills if I hadn't done this internship.

Luis' internship with a company that was client-focused helped him get the experience he needed to find the job he wants. His confidence grew because the company recognized his technical skills and used them in their business. And at the same time Luis was learning about the ups and downs of working with clients. The new people he met through his internship have become his network in job leads and free-lance work.

***

***

Jessica

Jessica realized that in her first internship at a county police depart-ment she really liked the work and training she did in cybercrime. She changed her major to cybercrime and Internet security because she knew that was the area for her.

Jessica took her second internship with a cybersecurity firm, and she knew she had a lot to learn.

My internship with a cybersecurity company was really an eye opener. I had so much to learn. I was always good at math and was pretty good with computers but realized I needed to be better. I worked really hard to learn everything and after the first weeks started to feel more comfortable.

Cyber situations change very fast. I felt there was always some-thing new to learn every week. The internship was challenging, but I loved it.

When I get my associate's degree I plan to go on to a university and get my bachelor's in digital and computer forensics. I want to use my skills in computer security and forensics analysis to work in a large police department or with Homeland Security. Interning at a real company has made me understand how important cybersecurity is in today's world.

This internship was really a challenge for me. But I'm really glad I did it. I was able to learn so much and so quickly that I feel confi-dent that I will find a job I will love in the future.

Jessica changed her major after her first year at community college because she knew she wanted to work in cybersecurity. She took on a challenging internship in her new field and worked hard to learn the skills she needed. And this experience helped her to know that she made the right decision.

***

ON A FINAL NOTE

If you're thinking about doing an internship, do it! Ask your school or college to help set one up for you. You'll be surprised to see how much you can learn and how much you can do in the real world.

Finding out about what you like—and what you don't like—now will make your future so much clearer. You'll make the decisions that are right for you because you know more about who you are and what you want.

Index

111, 114, 118, 128; résumé of,
36, 118, 137; supervisor meeting
with, 67–68; teamwork example
of, 56–57; Web design and, 9, 43

machines, office, 70–71
management: logistics, 112; time,
103, 104, 105
manager, Michelle's interview of,
121–22
meetings, 67–69, 72
mentor, 2, 67, 77–78, 97, 130
message taking, 70
Michelle: colleges and, 6, 116,
119, 122, 139–40; credit for,
13; deadline example of, 53–54;
elevator speech of, 29; guidance
counselor for, 6, 29, 65, 139;
internship of, 6, 13, 64–65,
89, 100, 127–28; interview of,
42, 53–54; job-related skills
of, 110–11; learned skills of,
110–11; manager interviewed
by, 121–22; new beginnings
for, 139–40; personal awareness
skills of, 115–16; projects of, 29,
53–54, 128; résumé of, 21–22,
33, 117–18, 133; transcript of,
119–20
Microsoft Project, 111, 117, 120

names, remembering of, 66
negative feelings, questions about,
56–60
nervousness, during interview,
43, 51
networking, 4, 132
new beginnings: for Alex, 140–41;
for Jessica, 142–43; for Luis,

141–42; for Michelle, 139–40;
right decisions made, 139–43
nonprofits, 4
normal cycles, of interns, 95
notes: project, 129; thank you,
126, 130

observing, 72
office machines, 70–71
office technology, 70–71
one-to-one interviews, 51
organizational structure, 84
organizations: in community, 4–5;
as internship term, 2
organizing. See planning and
organizing
overwhelming, internship as, 96

paperwork, 30–31
part-time work, 13–14, 22
passion, 7
pay: credit or, 13; for Luis, 12–13
personal awareness skills, 61, 117;
of Alex, 116; life skills, 113; of
Michelle, 115–16
placement services, 2, 22
planning and organizing skills,
113–15, 117, 121
portfolio, 122–23
positive attitudes, 38, 60, 126–27
post internship. See after internship
PowerPoint, 80, 110, 111, 117, 118
practice, for interview, 48–49
preparations, for interview
questions, 40–41
pride, 110, 132
prioritizing, 103, 104–5
problems, of internships, 96; with
being left out, 99–101; with

117, 121; projects relating to, 87, 88; soft, 38, 86; survival, 38, 86; for teamwork, 38. *See also* job-related skills; life skills; personal awareness skills
social media, 85
soft skills, 38, 86
speaking up, 106
specific questions, 53
speech. *See* elevator speech/pitch
sponsor, 2, 4, 19, 30–31
strong statement, with interview questions, 42
structure, organizational, 84
styles, of interviews, 51
subject lines, of e-mails, 23
success, of interview, 45–47
supervisors, 2; appointment with, 129; meetings with, 67–69; problems with, 97; questions about, 68–69
supplies, 69
survival skills, 38, 86

team, projects, 45
teamwork, 45, 46–47; internship relating to, 86, 87–88; Jessica's example of, 57–58; with life skills, 113, 121; Luis's example of, 56–57; skills for, 38
technology, office, 70–71
telephones: answering of, 70; during first few days, 69–70; interview by, 59
thank you e-mails, 23, 130
thank you notes, 126, 130

tie up loose ends, 127
time management, 103, 104, 105
time problems, 97
tips: on answering difficult or awkward questions, 59–61; for résumés, cover letters, cover e-mails, references, and e-mail addresses, 23–24
transcript, description of internship for, 119–20
transportation, 64–65

unpaid work, 22
updating, of résumés, 21, 117–19, 129–30, 133–37

vocabulary, 84–85
volunteer experience, 22

weakness, questions about, 61
Web design, Luis and, 9, 43
WordPress, 111
work, 81; assignment problems with, 97, 99; experience of, 39, 55; for family, 44; part-time, 13–14, 22; unpaid, 22. *See also* grunt work; networking; paperwork; teamwork
work ethics, 38, 45–46, 53–56, 86–88, 121
work expectations, 99; Alex's problem with, 102–3
work values inventories, 15
writing: of your own elevator speech/pitch, 30. *See also* résumé writing

About the Authors

Joan E. McLachlan launched her career with internships almost thirty years ago in New York City and has been working with students and school internship programs ever since.

She is director of Internship Quest, LLC, a company that provides consulting services and materials for quality internship programs.

Joan also works with the evaluation division of Measurement Incorporated on various educational research and evaluation projects and has been a consultant to the Nassau County (NY) High School Principals' Association's Senior Experience Network for over fifteen years.

She is coauthor of *Internships for Today's World: A Practical Guide For High Schools and Community Colleges.*

Joan is a graduate of Westminster College (BA); Hunter College (MS); and Pratt Institute (MLS). She currently resides in Centerville, Massachusetts, on Cape Cod.

Patricia Hess has over twenty-five years of experience in recruitment and management training. She has interviewed candidates for first-line positions and internships for global organizations.

She teaches organizational behavior at the University of Massachusetts, Dartmouth, at both the graduate and undergraduate levels.

Patricia is associate director of Internship Quest, LLC, (internshipquest.com) where she develops seminars and learning experiences to help students learn the behaviors, soft skills, and positive work attitudes and habits needed for successful employment.

She is coauthor of *Internships for Today's World: A Practical Guide for High Schools and Community Colleges.*

Patricia currently lives in Brewster on Cape Cod and is a graduate of Adelphi University (BA and MS) and Cass Business School City University, London (MBA).